Farewell lunch
13/06/17
from Joanna,
Fiona, Christiane,
Jane & Christiana

Aberdeenshire - A New Perspective

supported by

 Visit**Aberdeen**shire

This book is dedicated to Denis Law

A proud son of the city of Aberdeen, a hero and a friend.

First published in 2017 by Andy Hall Publishing. All photographs copyright to Andy Hall

The author can be contacted at www.andyhallphotography.com

ISBN 978-0-9955798-0-4

Designed by N & J Irvine, Perspectives - www.perspectivesnet.com

Aberdeenshire - A New Perspective

Images and Insights

Andy Hall

Foreword by Sir Ian Wood

A celebration of the City of Aberdeen and Aberdeenshire.

Acknowledgements

In the course of researching and producing **Aberdeen***shire - A New Perspective*, I have received assistance from a wide variety of sources. Primarily, my thanks go to all the contributors who have embraced the idea of the book with commitment and enthusiasm.

In addition to those who have been mentioned in the body of the publication, I would particularly like to acknowledge the following who have facilitated photographic opportunities, provided information and expedited communications. Without them, this publication would not exist.

Joe Law, Dave Macdermid of Aberdeen Football Club, Elma McMenemy of the Friends of Stonehaven Open Air Pool, Jim Wands of Dunnottar Castle, Bill Powrie, Lorraine Grant of The Barn, Chris Bain of Aberdeen Harbour Board, Rev. Stephen Taylor of the Kirk of St. Nicholas, Molly Imrie of TechFest, Adam McDougall of the National Theatre of Scotland, Craig Reekie of the Banchory Lodge Hotel, Ian McLaren of Innes Associates, Linzi Walker of Union Square, Jenny Brown of Aberdeen City Council (Lead Curator in History), Bethany Burns of BrewDog, Garry Marsden of Balmoral Estates, Paul Dobbie of Persuasion PR, Linsey Stewart and Michael Berry of the Scottish Government, Cameron and Team Hansen at the Hansen Residence, Ashley Simpson of Codona's, Mike Ward of the Grampian Transport Museum, Fred and Diane Bruce, Elaine Stephen of Cruden Bay Golf Club, Robert Gordon University, the University of Aberdeen, Michelle Slater of Glenglassaugh Distillery, Sally Borley of the National Trust for Scotland, Ellice Milton, Susan Sutherland of Maggie's Centre, Alistair Gunn, Rachael of Disbury of Deveron Projects, Alasdair Ross of Aberdeen City Council, Lynn Jeffrey of Beam Suntory, Danny Fitzgerald of Diageo Ltd, Laura Young of Whyte and Mackay Ltd, Louise Seaward of The Benriach Distillery Co. Ltd, Suzanne Clark of Bacardi Ltd, Margaret Mary Clarke of International Beverage Holdings Ltd, Christopher Swan Photography and Fiona Leese of JW Holdings Ltd.

My sincere thanks go to Sir Ian Wood for providing a foreword to this book. Sir Ian's encouragement of my work over several publications means a great deal to me.

My association with Perspectives (Niall and Jacqueline Irvine) who are responsible for the pre-production scanning and design of this book goes back 18 years. Their work is always outstanding. I'm delighted to be associated with their attention to detail, creative input, technical expertise and overall professionalism in achieving the quality that I need to represent my work. This includes, of course, Jacqueline's tomato soup which is second to none.

As I've mentioned elsewhere but I'd like to emphasise, I'm extremely grateful to have the support of Visit**Aberdeen**shire in providing the finance for this publication and, in particular, to have had the encouragement of my good friend Steve Harris, first Chief Executive of the organisation, which has been unstinting throughout.

Finally, my love and grateful thanks go to my wife Sylvia for her creative insight and the original idea for me to do this book. I'm very proud of it and hope that I've fulfilled the trust that everyone above has invested in me.

Foreword by Sir Ian Wood

Andy Hall is a genius at catching the optimum moment to capture scenes of beauty and the wonders of nature all around us, many of which we take for granted and walk by in our day to day lives.

Each of his previous books has become an acclaimed collection piece, preserving forever the beauty of many parts of Scotland and capturing many aspects of our diverse ways of life. This time, he's done it superbly for Aberdeen and Aberdeenshire.

This collection highlights much of the natural beauty and many different facets of life in our region, and Andy's persistence in waiting for the right moment to take the photograph produces some spectacular images.

He talks of rediscovering a vibrant and dynamic city with a unique cultural identity and a depth of talent in all its forms. He has done a great service to all of us and to posterity by capturing exactly that.

In this competitive world of international tourism, we're constantly looking for new ways to capture, present and market the beauty, the excitement, the simplicity, the variety, the hustle and bustle, the ethos, and the peace and solitude of where we live. That's exactly what Andy has done – not only with the photographs but with the accompanying narratives which outline the background to the images and describe the breathtaking splendour and majesty of some of nature's great wonders.

Thank you Andy for adding to your previous great works. This collection of wonderful images captures for posterity our region's natural beauty and Aberdeen's classical and contemporary architecture, together with the uniqueness and diversity of our widely varied way of life.

Andy Hall

Andy Hall's photographic reputation has gained international recognition as a result of the success of his books, *A Sense of Belonging to Scotland*, the favourite places of Scottish personalities, *Touched by Robert Burns* which was launched by Scotland's First Minister, the Rt. Hon. Alex Salmond, at Edinburgh Castle on St. Andrew's Night in 2008 and *Scotland's Still Light,* published in 2014 and launched at the Scottish Parliament in Edinburgh.

A Sense of Belonging to Scotland was used by former First Minister Jack McConnell for a ministerial visit to China. Ewan McGregor described it as *"The most beautiful collection of photographs of Scotland that I have ever seen!"*

Touched by Robert Burns was gifted to the nominees and judges of the Robert Burns Humanitarian Awards. Scotland's Still Light explored the relationship between photographic imagery and Scottish literature and has been used by Scotland's First Minister and her cabinet as a gift for visitors to and from Scotland.

Sir Alex Ferguson described *Scotland's Still Light - "Any photographic work by Andy Hall takes your breath away. This book demonstrates his love of Scotland and highlights the mystic beauty and raw energy of our country."*

Andy's most recent book entitled **Aberdeen***shire - A New Perspective* is about his native North East of Scotland. It reflects Aberdeen as a successful, attractive and vibrant city set within the beautifully atmospheric light of Aberdeenshire.

Network Aberdeen Social Enterprise

Since September 2013, I have been running my own business entitled Network Aberdeen to introduce the North East of Scotland to families who have come to live and work in the area.

My daughter Rebecca has autism and, now that she has left school, I've come to realise how few opportunities there are for young people with special needs like Rebecca's to have a meaningful working life.

In the light of Rebecca's special needs and those of others with a similar condition, I've been thinking for some time that I'd like to expand Network Aberdeen into a social enterprise company to give young people with additional support needs an opportunity to be meaningfully engaged in a real workplace environment.

When Andy described his publishing idea of **Aberdeen***shire - A New Perspective*, we thought that this could be the catalyst for an exciting opportunity for some local young adults with autism.

As a result, we have decided to form a partnership where Network Aberdeen Social Enterprise would be responsible for handling orders and distribution in a well-managed and structured workplace.

For ten years before his retirement from teaching in 2014, Andy worked with young people who had similar integration issues. He has a real understanding of the problems that they face.

With his photographic skills, publishing background and educational experience alongside my personal experience and business background, we are both very keen to be involved in a social enterprise project that will, hopefully, make a difference to the lives of some disadvantaged young people in our local area.

Dr. Caroline Traa

Introduction

I have lived in the North East of Scotland all my life. In that time, I have grown to love every aspect of it: the light, landscape, architecture, literature, music, history, nature and its people. When I embarked on the photography for this book, however, I wanted to see it with fresh eyes; to revisit the familiar, to discover the unfamiliar.

In the first year of retirement from teaching, I photographed four countries in nine months - the east coast of the United States, northern Italy, the magical Aegean island of Santorini and otherworldly Iceland. When I returned from my last trip, I decided that the time was right to explore my home area in more depth than I had done previously.

In my teaching of photography, I have two strong themes that I emphasise: begin on your doorstop and take time to absorb and distil your surroundings before composing and capturing the image. With an open brief and these two principles at the forefront of my mind, I set about exploring the city of Aberdeen and the diversity of surrounding Aberdeenshire, the places for which I have a real sense of belonging.

I resolved to explore well-trodden paths and roads less travelled. Hours of planning were invested in making sure that I made these journeys at the right time of day and in the right season to make the most of the quality and direction of light. This involved many unproductive days but I knew that by returning again and again, I would eventually be rewarded by the "decisive moment". Every return journey involved the same amount of planning and a renewed sense of anticipation. I'm a great believer in Louis Pasteur's maxim that "chance favours the prepared mind."

The next two years were a revelation to me. It became obvious very quickly that to photograph my home area at its best, I needed to render it in colour and in monochrome, depending on the subject's predominant characteristics.

I found myself setting up my tripod on rocks just off Pennan at 3.30am on Midsummer's Day, perching high above Union Street in December to capture its full length of Christmas lights and taking a portrait of a former pupil of mine who had reached the South Pole to become the first Scot and the youngest Brit to achieve such a feat.

The result is **Aberdeen**shire - *A New Perspective*. I'm indebted to Visit**Aberdeen**shire for its financial support and, in particular, first Chief Executive Steve Harris for encouraging me at every turn.

I also owe a debt of gratitude to the many contributors who have given their knowledge, writing skills and time to this project.

I'm delighted to be in partnership with Network Aberdeen Social Enterprise which my friend Dr. Caroline Traa has created to give young adults with additional support needs an opportunity to have a meaningful working experience.

I hope that I have produced something that we can all be proud of.

Andy Hall

Fit For A Local Hero

Pennan

Pennan is a village on the Moray Firth coast of Aberdeenshire that had fame thrust upon it in 1983 when it became the location for director Bill Forsyth's BAFTA-winning film Local Hero, produced by David Puttnam.

Starring Burt Lancaster, Peter Riegert, Peter Capaldi, Denis Lawson and Fulton McKay, the film reveals the story of a young executive of an American oil company who is sent to buy the fictional village of Ferness so that it can be be replaced by an oil refinery.

Fans from around the world come to Pennan to see the locations from the film. The village's most famous landmark is the traditional red telephone box that executive Mac used to call his Texas headquarters to relay the progress of his negotiations.

Denis Lawson, who played the part of Gordon Urquhart, the accountant and hotel owner in the film, recalls his role -

"It wasn't until I shot the movie Local Hero that my life took me to this beautiful part of the North East of Scotland. I remember arriving in Pennan the day before we were due to start shooting there. I walked around every part of it.

Since my character lived there, I wanted to get a real feel of the place. It didn't take long, of course, but since I'm from a small town myself (Crieff), I know what it's like to have an intimate knowledge of a whole village. My overriding memories are of how friendly and welcoming the local people were to the film unit and trying to complete a scene at night with only three hours of darkness!"

The only time that first light is directly on the north-facing village is at the Summer Solstice. The image opposite was taken at 4am on Midsummer's Day. The low light required a long exposure which, combined with the pastel characteristics and direction of the morning light, has rendered the scene with a soft, ethereal quality.

As with most villages on the Aberdeenshire coastline, the collection of whitewashed and colourful fishermen's cottages are built with their gables facing the sea to protect them from the elements. Whilst Pennan is often idyllic in summer, it is very dramatic in winter storms when waves crash on to the beach. The noise from the receding waves rushing through the multi-coloured pebbles can be deafening.

"The Northern Sky is a beautiful thing" says Burt Lancaster who plays Felix Happer, chief of the oil company in Local Hero and who has a fascination with astronomy. Ever-changing sunrises and sunsets cast changing light on the cottages of villages like Pennan and, with little or no light pollution, the night sky becomes a multitude of stars with the Aurora Borealis often a delightful occurrence.

Pennan at First Light, Midsummer

The Granite City

Heart Of Stone

Aberdeen is known as The Granite City. Examples of granite buildings can be seen all over Aberdeen from the most classical of monuments to the most unpretentious of buildings.

The North East of Scotland's geological base is granite. The stone has long been incorporated into local buildings and structures. The expansion of commerce and industry in the 18th century increased demand for granite. Greater traffic with iron-rimmed cartwheels increased the need for more durable road surfaces.

Granite was ideal for this and Aberdeen began to export the stone to other parts of the country including London. Aberdeen granite was used for the balustrade on Waterloo Bridge and in parts of the terracing of the Houses of Parliament.

Civil engineering projects such as harbour works and bridges further increased demand while merchants and manufacturers looked to granite to give them more imposing buildings and decorative features. Crucial to the expansion of the industry was Aberdeen's access to the sea with thousands of tons of stone transported through its harbour.

The single most significant breakthrough to working with granite came in the 19th century with the adoption of steam power. In the early 1830s, Alexander MacDonald designed a steam-driven polishing machine that revolutionised the production of polished granite slabs and made it economically feasible for relatively large-scale production to take place. MacDonald also devised a steam-powered saw and lathe. Gradually, the granite trade modernised and moved away from the old hand-crafted industry.

By the end of the 19th century, Aberdeen was the world centre for the granite trade. Quarries in the North East supplied the growing market for stone used in buildings, roads, sculptures and granite memorials. Granite yards were to be found throughout the city, the principal one being Rubislaw Quarry.

In 1964, Rubislaw Quarry provided stone for the KIng Robert the Bruce Memorial in Bannockburn and, later in the decade, Rubislaw granite was used to clad the podium of the Tower of London.

But the USA began to restrict imports of stone. New road-making materials, concrete and steel for building and the growing popularity of cremations all had a devastating impact on granite production. Despite granite yards introducing new machinery and amalgamating during the 20th century, it was not sufficient to save the industry.

By the 1970s, only a few working quarries remained and most of the yards closed. Rubislaw Quarry was the last granite quarry to close in 1971. A few manufacturers held on and can still be found turning out high quality work using a mix of the old craft skills and the latest technologies.

The War Memorial lion sculpture in Schoolhill, designed by William McMillan, is an excellent example of Aberdeen's granite heritage.

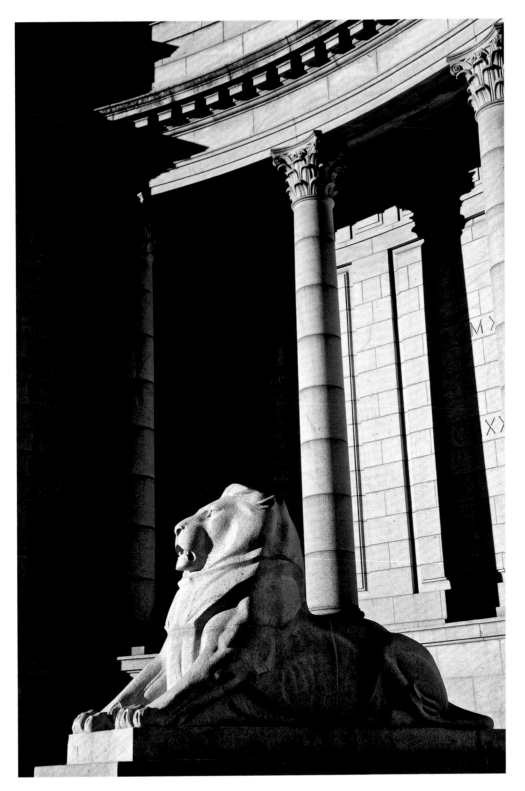

The War Memorial, Schoolhill

The Tread Of The Millennia

Bennachie

The unmistakable peak of Mither Tap on Bennachie dominates the central Aberdeenshire landscape. It is a symbol of homecoming for many North East people.

Cameron McNeish is an award-winning writer, television presenter and an Honorary Fellow of the Royal Scottish Geographical Society. He is very familiar with Bennachie and has climbed it many times -

"Bennachie broods and casts her spell over the fields and fairm touns of rural Aberdeenshire like the auld cailleach that she is. You can glimpse her crouching profile from the North Sea or from the high tops of the Cairngorms, a venerable and inscrutable presence who has known the tread of the millennia, from Bronze Age loons and well before."

The Bailies of Bennachie is a voluntary group formed in 1973 to help look after the hill. The Bailies keep very busy helping with practical management such as repairing footpaths and planting trees, assisting with research into the history and wildlife of the hill, and organising cultural events ranging from picnics to Doric Nights, from conceptual art projects to drama, based on local folklore, and publishing books about Bennachie.

Jill Matthews is a Bailie of Bennachie. She knows the iconic range of tops well -

"Conspicuous and standing proudly more than 1000ft above the surrounding farmland, the distinctive shape of Mither Tap draws the eye upwards; although it is but one of several tops on Bennachie (Gaelic origin Beinn-na-ciche meaning hill of the breast), it is a prominent, well-loved landmark for residents and travellers alike.

People have left their mark on Bennachie over millennia. The Iron Age fort is easily visible on Mither Tap, while many Pictish stones have been found in fields nearby. The remains of houses belonging to the Colonists scatter the slopes. These crofting people lived here for fifty years from 1800 onwards before they were forced off the land.

Nowadays, the open hilltops and the cloak of forests are hugely popular with visitors who enjoy walking, running and biking the network of paths.

The following is an extract from a poem by Daisy Bruce which appeared in The Book of Bennachie published by the Bailies of Bennachie in 1976.

And when we return from far off places
To where we have longed to be,
To the hills and the howes and the weel-kent faces,
We can glimpse our hill from the sea.
And then on the road, the homeward road
We face it full and plain,
And there we know as we gaze our fill,
We know we are home again.
For in every line of that old, dear hill
Lies all that means home to me.

Mither Tap, Bennachie

A City Of Gannets

Troup Head

Troup Head on the north Aberdeenshire coast, managed by RSPB Scotland, provides a breathtaking setting for the only mainland gannet colony in the country.

It offers unrivalled dramatic views along the Banffshire coast towards the Moray Firth. Birdwatchers visit from all over the world to witness tens of thousands of seabirds of a huge variety of species in their natural habitats.

The cliffs are almost deserted in winter but the first gannets return to the cliffs from mid-January onwards. By spring, tens of thousands of seabirds have arrived, including gannets and puffins.

In summer, fulmars, gannets, guillemots, razorbills, kittiwakes and herring gulls crowd on to the cliffs while smaller numbers of puffins nest in burrows or crevices. Shags, eiders and the occasional great skua can be seen just off-shore. The cliff-top is swathed in thrift and campions. Out to sea, bottle-nosed dolphins and porpoises can often be spotted. Grey and common seals are seen regularly.

Gannets are fascinating to watch. They are extremely fast in flight and accurate in their fishing technique. With wings tightly tucked in, they identify their targets from a great height and accelerate vertically into the sea at speeds of approaching 60 miles per hour to capture their next meal.

On making contact with the water, gannets trigger inflated bags of air around their necks and throats to absorb the force of impact. The speed of the dive can plunge them 15 metres under the water, their eyes protected by specially-adapted membranes. The submerged fish are captured with serrated beaks and are only consumed after surfacing.

Other RSPB sites in Aberdeenshire are Fowlsheugh, just south of Stonehaven, and the Loch of Strathbeg near Fraserburgh. The spectacular cliffs at Fowlsheugh are packed with 130,000 breeding seabirds in spring and summer. The Loch of Strathbeg is Britain's largest dune loch. In winter, thousands of wild geese, swans and ducks fly in, including 20 per cent of the world's population of pink-footed geese.

Gannets are a photographer's dream, particularly when engaged in the courtship ritual of "billing". Their distinctive blue-rimmed eyes and the pastel yellow shading of their necks, captured at the point of their bills touching, is a prize that many photographers seek for their portfolios.

By discreetly using a long lens so as not to disturb the intimate activity, I was able to position myself to allow the background of the similarly-coloured sea to complement the eye-colour of the birds.

When I returned along the cliff path having captured the image opposite, I slowed to talk to a fellow photographer. I hadn't realised initially that he was French. When I enquired of him what he thought of the gannet display, he replied with one word - *"Magnifique!"*

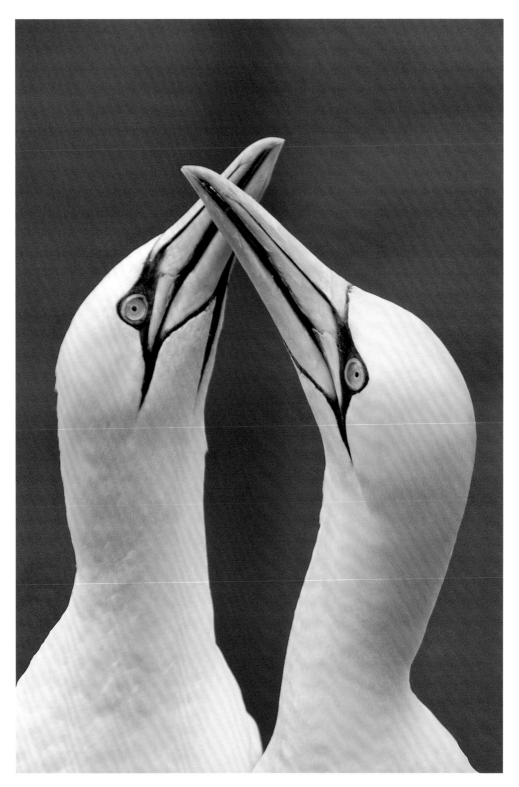

Billing Gannets, Troup Head

Theatre Of Dreams And Memories

Pittodrie

Pittodrie Stadium is the home of Aberdeen Football Club and has been since its formation in 1903. It has a special place in the hearts of North East football supporters and has seen many memorable games over the past eleven decades.

I have been a Dons fan since my first game at Pittodrie, a 2-1 defeat against Dunfermline Athletic on the 21st of January 1967 when the late Ernie Winchester scored the only Aberdeen goal. Every week, I'd wait at the players' entrance to get a close-up glimpse of my heroes and a few words with them in pursuit of a precious signature.

Those players assumed a godlike status, none more so than Jinky Smith, King of the Nutmeg (pushing the ball through an opponent's legs to gain an advantage). I can still recall the team from the early days managed by the inspirational Eddie Turnbull - Clark, Whyte, Shewan, Munro, McMillan, Petersen, Storrie, Smith, Johnston, Melrose and Wilson - the team sheet indelibly printed on my memory.

Since then my favourites have been Joey Harper, Willie Miller and Gordon Strachan for their respective qualities of record goalscoring, world-class penalty box defending and creative genius.

One game, in particular, will stand out forever for those who were lucky enough to have been there - the evening of March 16th, 1983, Pittodrie's greatest night. On the club's unforgettable journey to winning the European Cup Winners' Cup against Real Madrid on a rainy night in Gothenburg that year, the Dons welcomed Bayern Munich to Pittodrie for the second leg at the quarter-final stage, after a very creditable 0-0 draw at the Olympic Stadium in Munich.

Bayern's team contained many world-class players including Karl-Heinz Rummenigge and Paul Breitner. Masterminded by Alex Ferguson, now Sir Alex Ferguson, Aberdeen secured a famous 3-2 victory in the return leg in front of a capacity crowd of 24,000.

In his autobiography The Don, inspirational captain Willie Miller remembers - *"It remains my favourite Pittodrie encounter and nothing comes close. It was a victory to cherish, the most intense atmosphere that I have ever experienced at Pittodrie. I still get a tingle in my spine when I remember the din made by the crowd at the final whistle - and Fergie's little dance on to the pitch."*

The stadium is particularly magical in an evening game under floodlights. When the Dandy Dons are attacking in full-flight, the atmosphere generated by the fans is magnificent, encapsulated in the image opposite with Graeme Shinnie bearing down on goals.

Although its future is uncertain and there are plans for a new stadium, Pittodrie will always remain in the hearts and memories of Dons supporters all over the world.

Pittodrie by Floodlight

21st Century Learning

The Sir Duncan Rice Library

The Sir Duncan Rice Library at the University of Aberdeen is a 21st Century space for learning and research. It was officially opened on the 24th of September 2012 by Her Majesty Queen Elizabeth II. It houses the largest of the University's modern collections on Floors 1-7, including Arts, Humanities, Sciences and Social Sciences, and historic collections of rare books, manuscripts and archives in the Special Collections Centre on the Lower Ground Floor.

The University of Aberdeen is the 5th oldest English language university in the world. The new library serves a community of 14,000 students, containing 1,200 reading spaces from traditional silent study rooms to interactive areas for collaborative projects, supported by information technology.

Professor Sir Duncan Rice is a Scottish academic who was Principal of the University of Aberdeen from 1996 until 2010. He was previously Vice-Chancellor at New York University in the United States. His premise was that great universities have great libraries. He wanted this one to be the most vibrant centre of university life, and to be a monumental piece of architecture which would symbolise the greatness of the university, in much the same way as Elphinstone envisaged the chapel five hundred years and more before.

Sir Duncan also wanted the library plaza to unite the campus on the landward side of the High Street, and to reflect the pattern of squares formed by the older buildings on its seaward side.

The Library is designed as one large rectangular cuboid. Visual lightness and airiness in combination with its proportionality, materials palette and clean lines lend the building a timeless quality. A large organic opening that cuts through the floors at every level creates continuous visual connections throughout the full height of the building. The atrium is the central hub.

Consisting of an irregular pattern of insulated panels and high performance glazing, the façade shimmers during the day and glows softly at night, creating a luminous landmark for Aberdeen.

At the opening of the £57 million pound building, Principal Sir Ian Diamond said *"Our students will be able to access, through electronic means, all the collections that exist all over the world. The very best students will want to come to Aberdeen to study here in this incredible environment."*

The building, designed by Danish architects Schmidt Hammer Lassen, was conceived to symbolise the ice and light of the north. The design concept was to provide *"a meeting place and a cultural centre for the University and the wider Aberdeen community."*

The year after it was opened, the Library won the Royal Incorporation of Architects in Scotland (RIAS) Award as well as the Royal Institute of British Architects (RIBA) National Award.

In reflecting on being honoured in this way, Sir Duncan Rice has said, *"Not surprisingly for an Aberdeen graduate whose family has been largely made up of Aberdeen graduates, I find it hard to imagine any greater honour than having the library carry my name."*

The Sir Duncan Rice Library, University of Aberdeen

Grampian Eye Big Wheel, Codonas Amusement Park

Christmas on Union Street

South Pole Hero

Luke Robertson

In 1995, during my period as Head Teacher of Netherley School, I enrolled a bright young pupil named Luke Robertson into Primary 5. Little did I know then that, twenty years later, he would be the first solo Scot and youngest British-born explorer to cross Antarctica and reach the South Pole!

Luke recalls his incredible journey -

"On December 5th 2015, I set off on my skis from Hercules Inlet at the very edge of Antarctica. Dragging only my 130kg sledge for company, I was aiming to become the first Scot to ski 730 miles to the South Pole, completely alone.

Following recent health issues, I was also seeking to inspire others to set out to achieve their own goals in life, and not just dream about doing so. As I set up my tent on the very first evening, the weather was clear, the air clean and crisp, and the sun shone high in the southern polar sky. This was indeed that wild, raw and beautiful perfect place that I had sought.

The very next day, however, the weather turned and I soon saw the other side of Antarctica. For the following six weeks, I found myself battling against strong headwinds, unseasonably deep snow and temperatures reaching minus 60C.

Hunger, hallucinations, exhaustion and dehydration all took their toll in their own indomitable way and each step became both physically and psychologically draining. Although the prospect of not succeeding was my biggest fear, it also became my biggest motivation to prevail.

Finally, on January 13th 2016, I took the last few aching steps to reach the bottom of the world, the South Pole. I felt so so humbled by those who had helped me get there - in particular my wife, Hazel - and those intrepid explorers who had set foot there over 100 years prior to me."

Sir Ranulph Fiennes praised Luke's achievement - *"Reaching the South Pole, solo and unassisted, was, without doubt, one of the most enduring challenges possible and I am delighted to have supported Luke in all his efforts to become the youngest Brit ever to do so, unaided. It is an incredible achievement and I hope that his adventure inspires others to achieve their own goals in life and to raise funds for Marie Curie – a charity also close to my heart."*

Since his return, Luke has done many talks in aid of Marie Curie Nurses about his adventure. He discusses his life-changing set of circumstances following brain and heart surgery at a young age and the determination and ambition to take on challenges both from a physical and psychological perspective in all aspects of life.

Luke's website is www.lukerobertson.org. It is an amazing story of inspiration, motivation and achievement.

Luke Robertson

Where Education And Industry Meet

Robert Gordon University

Walking through the Garthdee campus of Robert Gordon University is a delight from an architectural and landscape perspective.

Professor Ferdinand von Prondzynski is Principal and Vice-Chancellor. He explains the history and the local and global importance of the university to the city of Aberdeen -

"When the businessman Robert Gordon, who had returned to North East Scotland from making his fortune in Danzig, founded Robert Gordon's Hospital in 1729, he cannot have imagined how far the institution would travel over the centuries. Two other major benefactors helped to make RGU what it is today: John Gray, who in the 19th century endowed what is today Gray's School of Art; and Tom Scott Sutherland, who made a gift of the Garthdee Estate in 1955, thereby giving the university what is now its main campus.

Today, Robert Gordon University is recognised as an extraordinarily innovative institution. Over the years, it has introduced pioneering teaching methods, research that continues to find solutions to the problems faced by society or by industry, and engagement with the city and region that has helped to transform it for the better. In 2012, it started the process that has led to the Aberdeen City Centre Masterplan, and subsequently it has led initiatives to sustain and develop the regional economy. It has been a strong and reliable friend and partner to the other educational institutions in the North East.

RGU's Garthdee campus is one of the most striking in the UK. It runs along the River Dee and includes both beautiful landscaping that is a legacy from the old Garthdee estate and buildings of great architectural merit. Gray's School of Art is housed in a noted modernist building modelled on the Illinois Institute of Technology. The Aberdeen Business School is in a striking structure designed by the renowned architect Norman Foster.

The newest building on the campus, the Sir Ian Wood Building (pictured here), is one of the most exciting structures in Aberdeen, with generous open interior spaces and wonderful views over the river and the city. The campus also houses a health and social care building, a well used sports centre, and the historic Victorian Garthdee House, the old manor house of the estate.

Today all of RGU's students are taught in Garthdee. The university still owns the old administration building in the city centre (on a site it shares with Robert Gordon's College, which is also descended from Robert Gordon's Hospital), but the beating heart is in Garthdee. Here it undertakes its teaching and research, but it also reaches out to the local community of which it is a proud part.

RGU also connects Aberdeen with the wider world – students from every continent come to study here and return to their countries as ambassadors of North East Scotland. Go to a meeting with businesspeople in Houston, Lagos or Perth (Australia), and the chances are that you'll be meeting RGU alumni. Not long from now, RGU will be 300 years old: it will have much to celebrate."

The Sir Ian Wood Building, Robert Gordon University

"A Journey To Another World!"

Stonehaven Harbour

I have lived in Stonehaven for the best part of fifty years. Whenever I return from being away from home, I walk up the Bervie Braes to look down on the picturesque harbour.

The Shorehead (harbour front) is a lively place to be in the summer with the Marine Hotel and the Ship Inn providing refreshment and sustenance for local people and visitors alike. From my youth, I've enjoyed sitting outside one or other of the establishments having a drink with friends on a summer's evening.

Most Sunday mornings, I walk around the harbour with my camera. I always find it to be a treasure trove of photographic subjects: abstract images with reflected light, rusty chains, patterns in the sand, silhouettes of creels and colourful nets and buoys piled randomly in heaps around the quayside.

For me, Stonehaven Harbour is one of many jewels in Aberdeenshire's crown. In the first hour of a sunny summer's morning, as in the image opposite, it's not too difficult for me to imagine that I'm in Cornwall or in the south of France.

The glory days for Stonehaven Harbour arrived with the boom in the herring industry of the 19th Century. In response to this, the harbour was significantly rebuilt. The South Pier was constructed by Robert Stevenson, the famous engineer and grandfather of writer Robert Louis Stevenson.

These were bountiful days but it was not to last. As with many other ports, the fishing industry of Stonehaven went into long-term decline. Operational vessels were in single figures by the final decade of the 20th Century and today a walk around the harbour reveals that pleasure craft are the principal occupants to be berthed in the inner and outer harbours.

Denis Law, Scotland's greatest-ever footballer, grew up in Aberdeen but Stonehaven played a large part in his young life before leaving for Huddersfield to begin his career in football as a fifteen year old -

"When I was a young boy, I couldn't wait for our family bus trips to Stonehaven. It was like a journey to another world! My Dad was a trawlerman sailing out of Aberdeen Harbour so the coast has always been very important to me. Much as I love the city of Manchester, I've always had an emotional connection to the sea.

A trip to Stonehaven was huge for us as a family - like having the Mediterranean Riviera only sixteen miles away. I remember visiting the Open Air Pool and Dunnottar Castle and thinking that they were wonderful but it is the harbour area that still draws me back every time I return to the North East.

Stonehaven is always on my mind and I have a real sense of anticipation before seeing the harbour again. Andy's image captures it perfectly."

Stonehaven Harbour Morning

Gateway To The North Sea

Aberdeen Harbour

Aberdeen Harbour is one of the UK's busiest ports and represents a vital part of Scotland's infrastructure. It plays a key role in Europe's energy sector, supports lifeline ferry services to the Northern Isles and has commercial trading links to around 40 countries across the world.

The harbour also has a fascinating history. According to the Guinness Book of Business Records, it is the oldest existing business in Britain since King David I of Scotland first granted the Bishop of Aberdeen the right to levy a tithe on all ships trading at the harbour in 1136.

Over the centuries, trade in animal hides, ceramics, shipbuilding, textiles, fishing and global transportation of granite from the city's famous quarries have all relied on the facilities of this essential North Sea gateway.

The port has witnessed record levels of activity in recent years and is key to sustaining the commercial growth of the region.   It is the centre of activity for offshore oil and gas industry marine support in North West Europe and a marshalling point for oilfield exports. North Sea oil has ensured the Granite City's strategic role in the fortunes of the Scottish and UK economies.

As well as being key to the energy sector, the harbour is the principal mainland port for passenger, freight and livestock services to Orkney and Shetland and is a port-of-call for cruise ships, a sector which is about to expand significantly.

With around £200 million invested by the Harbour Board in recent decades, the evolution of the port is ongoing and is aimed at meeting the changing requirements of existing users and of accommodating new activity and potential markets.

Major developments of recent years have included the multi-million pound development of facilities at the Torry Marine Base where a deep-water, state-of-the-art quayside was completed in 2014.

Looking to the future, the Harbour Board has recently announced commencement of a £350 million project to expand facilities at Aberdeen Harbour at neighbouring Nigg Bay that will allow existing customers to diversify and expand their interests whilst attracting new customers. These will include increased decommissioning activity, a more significant share of the larger cruise ship market and being able to accommodate much larger commercial vessels.

At the announcement of the new plans, Alistair Mackenzie, Chairman of Aberdeen Harbour Board, stated, *"We believe that the infrastructure developed at Nigg Bay will encourage and support the continued prosperity of the city and region that the harbour serves and make a significant national economic contribution."*

Scheduled to be completed by 2020, the development was welcomed by Minister for Transport and the Islands, Humza Yousaf, who added, *"These are exciting times for Aberdeen Harbour. I wish everyone involved in the project every success."*

Harbour Lights, Aberdeen

Innovative, Diverse And Creative

The Barn

The Barn is a nationally recognised contemporary arts centre based in Banchory, in rural Aberdeenshire. It is governed by Woodend Arts Limited, a registered Scottish Charity. An inspirational and welcoming space, the Barn offers a diverse cultural programme for all ages – encompassing theatre, music, film, dance, comedy, talks and visual art. It attracts 20,000 visitors a year. A collaborative team of staff, artists and 50 volunteers work together to devise and deliver an annual programme of 150 performances and 200 creative workshops, ensuring that rural audiences can enjoy access to high-quality work from the best national and local artists and performers.

For over 20 years, the Barn has championed environmental and ecological awareness, including the creation of a wild garden and 110 community allotments, positively influencing the lifelong learning and wellbeing of local residents. Creative projects frequently explore the connections between art, the environment and sustainability.

With a growing national reputation for cutting-edge creativity, the Barn plays a key role in supporting artists at all career stages to create and develop new work through a series of ongoing residencies, commissions and research projects within the local community.

The image opposite of is of a very memorable concert by MOBO award-winners Sons of Kemet and, specifically, their saxophonist Shabaka Hutchings. They provided an evening that spanned jazz, rock, African music and Caribbean folk. The Sons of Kemet concert is a typical example of the imaginative, diverse programming of the Barn's creative team.

Personally, I have attended many events at the Barn over the years. I've enjoyed art exhibitions from a variety of genres and have exhibited there myself in a series of monochrome photographic images entitled Celtic Stills.

I have been absorbed by theatre performances, one of which, Hector, tells the true story of the Scottish hero "Fighting Mac", Sir Hector Macdonald, who rose from humble beginnings as a crofter's son through the ranks of the British Army to become a knight of the realm and ultimately died a tragic death in Paris. The Barn performance of Hector was unforgettable.

I have been delighted by a range of musical talent from KT Tunstall to The Hayseed Dixies. My most recurring visits have been to see and hear highland fiddler Duncan Chisholm. In excellent acoustics, Duncan's plaintive music hung in the air like a singing voice. Scottish Opera is also part of the diverse musical offerings.

Comedy acts appear regularly on the programme along with carefully selected arthouse films; one that I attended on impressionist painter Renoir was screened to a very appreciative audience.

In the cultural lives of North East arts lovers, the Barn plays a central role. Its continuing success means that innovation, diversity and creativity will be available in Aberdeenshire for many years to come.

Sons Of Kemet

A Strategic Fortress

Dunnottar Castle

As a landscape photographer, few places have captured my imagination as much as Dunnottar Castle, a mile or so south of my home town of Stonehaven. As local people know and as visitors discover, it sits on an isolated outcrop of pudding-stone rock, making it one of the most impregnable fortresses to exist in Scotland.

Surrounded by sea on three sides but now in ruins, its defensive qualities of years gone by can still be readily appreciated and its colourful history floods the imagination when viewing it in a variety of moods.

Dunnottar has played many important roles in Scottish history and was even the setting for Franco Zeffirelli's Hamlet in 1990 starring Mel Gibson, Glenn Close and Helena Bonham-Carter.

Saint Ninian, an early missionary among the Pictish peoples, built a place of worship at Dunnottar in the 4th Century AD and, in 1276, a new stone church was consecrated for worship by William Wishart, the Bishop of St Andrews, on the site of Ninian's chapel.

A Scottish force in 1297 under William Wallace captured the castle. The English garrison inside took refuge in the church but Wallace burned it with the soldiers inside, destroying the fortress.

Mary Queen of Scots visited the castle for the first time in 1562. She returned two years later with her young son, the future James VI. James VI returned to the castle eighteen years later and spent ten days there, hunting deer on nearby estates, carrying out court duties and enjoying the hospitality of the Keith family. He visited many times thereafter.

Possibly the most significant historical event, though, took place in 1652 in what became known as the Saving of Scotland's Honours. Oliver Cromwell's army had laid siege to capture the Scottish Regalia (Scotland's Crown Jewels). The castle held out for eight months. Heavy cannons arrived in 1652 and on the 24th of May that year, surrender was made.

This was not, however, before the Honours of Scotland were smuggled out of the castle in a creel covered in seaweed by Mrs. Grainger, wife of the minister at Kinneff, a parish several miles south, and taken to Kinneff Church. They remained hidden there until the restoration of the monarchy in 1660 and were returned to Edinburgh Castle where they remain to this day.

Hollywood and Shakespearean actor Brian Cox recalls a vivid childhood memory - *"I first went to Dunnottar Castle on a school trip. I couldn't believe it. It was so dramatic and almost fairy-like. I remember it was so dark in winter. Dunnottar had a haunting effect on me which has never left me."*

Of all the photographs that I have taken of the castle over the years, this is my favourite. Low, late-afternoon light on the snow-blasted walls makes Dunnottar in winter an unforgettable experience to witness.

Dunnottar in Winter

Black Gold In A Silver City

The Oil Industry

When trying to represent visually the importance of the oil industry to Aberdeen's economic history over the past 50 years, the Oil Industry Chapel stained glass window in the Kirk of St.Nicholas in Aberdeen captivated me in its colour, vibrancy and design. It is the work of Shona McInnes -

"This photograph is a detail from the stained glass window that I designed and made in 1989 to mark the 25th anniversary of North Sea Oil and is an oasis of calm in the busy city centre.

In this detail of the window are today's harvesters of the sea - the oil tankers, support vessels and supply boats which service the exploration and production fields, symbolised by platforms set against the background of an open sea, darkening towards the horizon.

Here, vibrant red and green glass jewels sparkle against deep cobalt and Prussian blues, each jewel representing one of the oil and gas fields which were in production when the window was designed. A white jewel commemorates the Piper Alpha field.

In over thirty years of making stained glass, this has always been one of my favourite windows. It still makes me draw breath upon entering the chapel and has the same impact and vibrancy as the day it was installed. I used a lot of intense blue in this window, a colour which which works wonderfully in the cold north light, bathing the chapel in a calm, ethereal glow."

To place the window in the context of the bigger picture of the oil industry's development in the area, Deirdre Michie, Chief Executive of Oil and Gas UK, explains -

"This beautiful stained glass window records the North Sea oil and gas industry, shows its links with Aberdeen and pays tribute to all those who have worked in the sector. While the window marks 25 years of exploration and production on the UK Continental Shelf, the industry has played a prominent role in the lives of people in the North East of Scotland for 50 years.

The UK oil and gas industry remains a significant contributor to the regional economy, supporting skilled jobs and contributing entrepreneurial flair. Aberdeen and the North East is now a centre of excellence where the expertise, services and products developed by local companies are in demand all around the world.

Captured here are the key elements that underpin the industry's ability to rise to its challenges: its amazing engineering ingenuity, the ability to recover billions of barrels of oil from a challenging offshore environment and the sheer scale of operations required to achieve this amazing feat. These qualities have served this industry well and will ensure that it continues to have a sustainable future in the North East and the UK for many years to come."

The Oil Industry Chapel, Kirk of St. Nicholas

A Celebration Of Global Talent

Aberdeen International Youth Festival

Each year, at the end of July and at the beginning of August, the North East is awash with vibrant colour and reverberates with the energy of the Aberdeen International Youth Festival (AIYF). Stewart Aitken, its Artistic Director and CEO, describes the festival's cultural importance -

"The Aberdeen International Youth Festival began in the early 1970s with the aim of bringing young musicians and performing artists from across the world to meet, share, collaborate and perform in the city and the wider North East of Scotland. Over the many years that the festival has been a key cultural event, this desire to celebrate and learn from each other about the diverse cultures and the common love of creativity and performing has remained at its heart.

Since 1973, AIYF has welcomed nearly 40,000 young people and their artistic teams to the region with representatives from 100 different countries including all genres of music, dance and theatre as well as circus troupes, film and visual artists and street performers.

The festival is produced by a small core staff that is supported by over 50 summer festival staff and volunteers, a number of whom return each year. The volunteers, both backroom and those working directly with the visiting groups, provide a crucial component to the success of the event for participants and audiences alike with their local knowledge, enthusiasm and dedication.

Support is also received from many people across the region who welcome the performers to their venues and are advocates for the event and cultural life of the region. AIYF also benefits from very generous investment from local companies across many sectors as well as public funding, most notably from Aberdeen City Council.

AIYF has presented performers from many continents and the annual programme of activity includes major concerts in the city arts venues, daytime concerts in community-based venues, concerts and variety gala events across the North East, an education programme, social events and free events in the community and city centre like "Festival in the City.

The pictured Angklung Orchestra is a wonderful example of the diverse and high-quality groups that participate and, in many cases, return to AIYF to experience the welcome and the platform to perform, share and collaborate at one of the largest youth multi-arts festivals in the world."

Councillor George Adam, Lord Provost of Aberdeen and Patron of Aberdeen International Youth Festival, reflects on the place of the event in the city's cultural calendar -

"AIYF has filled Aberdeen's summers with the sights and sounds of the world for over forty years. The festival is an international stage for the brightest young performers and an inspiration to participants, audiences, and the local community. At a time when global relations are strained, AIYF continues to bring diverse groups of people together to celebrate the things we all have in common."

The Aberdeen International Youth Festival

The Cairngorms National Park

The Earl Of Mar's Punchbowl

The Cairngorms National Park, particularly in winter, is one of the most spectacular and challenging environments in the world. As well as being a diverse habitat for wildlife and plants, it has a fascinating history.

Brian Wood, Deputy Convener of the Cairngorms National Park Board explains the valuable significance of the Park and a famous Jacobite legend that has passed down through generations on Royal Deeside -

"Enclosing an area almost twice the size of Luxembourg, the Cairngorms National Park is by far the largest of the UK's national parks. Established in 2003 with the primary aim of conserving and enhancing the natural and cultural heritage of the area, it is one of the most spectacular locations on the planet. National Geographic Traveller Magazine has voted it one of the top twenty places in the world to visit.

Within the boundary of the Cairngorms are four of the UK's highest peaks – Ben Macdui, Braeriach, Cairntoul and Cairngorm with the Park providing shelter and protection for 25% of the UK's rarest and most endangered species from capercaillie to golden eagle and from wildcat to pine marten. It is a Mecca for outdoor activities enthusiasts with almost two million visitors flocking to the Park each year to enjoy the scenery, the wildlife, the castles, the food and the challenge of the mountains.

Three hundred years ago, the Cairngorms was the backdrop for one of the more colourful events in Scottish history. In September 1715, at the Linn of Quoich, John Erskine, 6th Earl of Mar and John Farquharson of Invercauld, Chief of Clan Farquharson, gathered together a band of Jacobite sympathisers from across the Highlands on the pretext of a hunting expedition. In fact they were plotting to overthrow the unpopular German-born, Protestant King George I and return the House of Stuart to the throne of Britain.

Legend has it that the Earl filled a hole in a nearby rock, now known as the Earl of Mar's Punchbowl, with locally produced liquor and the men drank to the health of the exiled King James VII, The King across the Water. Days later, they raised their standard in the village of Braemar and so began the ill-fated 1715 Jacobite Rising which was to wither soon afterwards on the battlefields of Sheriffmuir."

The image opposite is of the Earl of Mar's Punchbowl. Using a long exposure for the fast flowing River Quoich, it conveys the ethereal quality of the moving water contrasted with the patterned detail on the rocks and in the scattered pine needles.

A word of caution to photographers, though. The rocks can be very slippy so a telephoto lens from a distance on a tripod would be the best and safest way to capture this unusual and atmospheric location with its royal associations.

The Earl of Mar's Punchbowl, Linn of Quoich

Castlegate Abstract

The Mirrored Pavillion

I love abstract photography. When I first saw the Mirrored Pavilion in the Castlegate, I was attracted to it like a magnet. I came to realise that this imaginative installation was there to celebrate both the Festival of Architecture in 2016 and the Look Again Visual Art and Design Festival.

Look Again's festival director is Sally Reaper. Sally explains the background to the Mirrored Pavilion -

"It is hard to believe that the Mirrored Pavilion was designed by a young North East architecture student. The glittering structure was the brainchild of 20-year old Lucy Fisher from Robert Gordon University (RGU).

Beating off stiff competition to win a creative challenge set by organisers of the inaugural Look Again festival in 2015, Lucy and her peers joined forces with local architects and contractors to take her pavilion from a simple sketch to an inspiring live project.

Despite facing some logistical challenges - brought about mainly by torrential rainfall during the build - the team constructed the giant pavilion in less than one week. Designed on a 5m by 7m wooden frame, its outer skin was painstakingly decorated with thousands of tiny resin squares, reflecting the area's stunning architecture – as well as the daily hustle and bustle of city life.

The temporary structure dominated the pedestrianised square in the lead up to the five-day Look Again festival, creating a buzz of excitement and increased footfall to this historic spot. The Mirrored Pavilion perfectly embodied the very nature of the Look Again festival – a celebration of the talent in the North East, a commitment by the city to invest in emerging artists and an invitation to everyone to come and enjoy visual art and design.

Spearheaded by RGU and Aberdeen-based art agency SMART, Look Again is a groundbreaking festival, already rivalling some of the top festivals in the UK. Hundreds of visitors and city residents take part in the annual celebration, which includes a diverse range of workshops, talks and exhibitions. Showcasing world-renowned artists, as well as budding young talent, Look Again encourages us all to take a second look at our surroundings."

After graduating from Gray's School of Art, Sally trained at the prestigious Slade School of Art in London before returning to the North East to launch SMART. Pursuing her dream of putting the region on the map for visual art and design, Sally and her team are committed to supporting and promoting emerging creatives on their artistic journey.

On the day that I discovered The Mirrored Pavilion with my camera, I walked round it several times, engrossed in the million different reflections of Aberdeen appearing on its undulating surface. I eventually positioned myself to photograph the busy junction of King Street and Union Street and waited for a colourful bus to sweep round the corner!

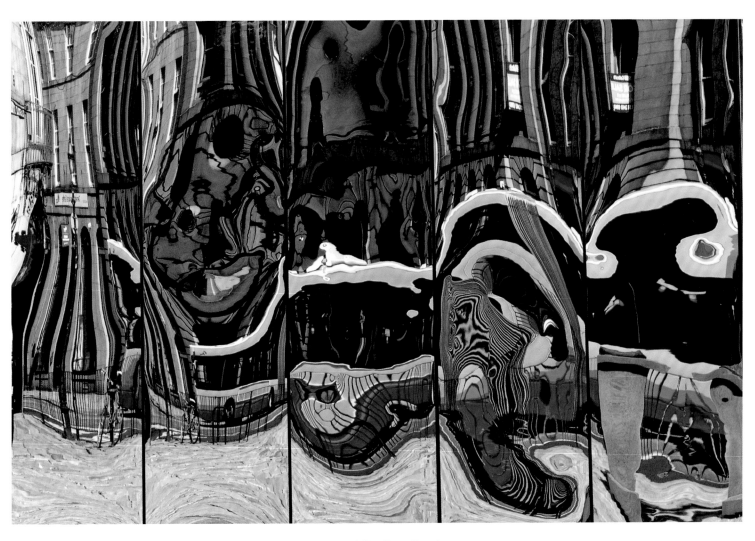

The Mirrored Pavilion, Castlegate

Harvesting The Sea

The Fishing Industry

Mike Park is Chief Executive of the Scottish White Fish Producers Association. He joined the board twenty years ago and progressed up through the ranks to become Chairman in 2004; he became Chief Executive in 2008.

Mike's successful fishing career has spanned thirty years with twenty five of those as skipper and vessel owner. In this piece, he reflects on the changes that have taken place in the fishing industry in the North East of Scotland and how it has been part of his life since boyhood -

"Fishing has changed significantly over the last century. From a very basic, rugged and physically challenging profession during the days of sail and steam, modern vessels are now powered by the most efficient diesel engines, have the latest technology for hauling the nets and have access to the finest communication systems.

Vessels now navigate the seas and find the shoals of fish with technology that only a decade ago was seen as futuristic. Changed days from the time when the wives followed the drift net fleets around the UK coast gutting the herring and baiting the haddock lines; in those days fishing was seen as a way of surviving rather than a means to prosperity.

My own fishing career started as a cocksure and enthusiastic young lad in short trousers in the small fishing village of Stonehaven, just to the south of Aberdeen. Staying at the very front of the harbour, I could monitor every event, the sailing of the vessels to the grounds and their return to harbour with fish laid out on the deck in the wooden boxes.

Catching the ropes as the vessel docked alongside the quay was my proud responsibility as was helping them clean (gut) the last of the fish before they were dispatched to the fish market in Aberdeen. From there, I grew to love the sea and love fishing. By the age of twenty one, I was skipper of my own twenty five-metre trawler and at twenty five built a state of the art vessel at Miller's boat yard in St Monans in Fife.

My best Christmas present ever in terms of being euphoric was a set of oilskins at the age of nine; they came in extremely handy during a six-week fishing trip on a great-line vessel to Rockall Bank soon after. Those were the days, little fear, great enthusiasm and a huge desire to succeed in the industry I had come to love."

The image opposite is Fraserburgh Harbour on a beautiful April morning. Fraserburgh is ideally positioned for the fishing grounds of the north and east of Scotland. The location makes it well placed for trade with Scandinavia and the Baltic sea ports.

The serried ranks of gleaming, colourfully-painted trawlers waiting to disgorge their catches are a sight to behold.

Fraserburgh Harbour Morning

Inspiring Scientists Of The Future

TechFest Science Festival

TechFest is a charitable organisation whose aim is to promote Science, Technology, Engineering, and Maths (STEM). The flagship event in September is the North East of Scotland's annual science festival.

In 2016, the new Eureka Family Science Series was launched, allowing a greater variety of dynamic workshops and events for families to enjoy across Aberdeen City and Aberdeenshire. Taking place after school, the Eureka Series toured libraries giving children of all ages the chance to experience thought-provoking hands-on activities, with parents and grandparents welcome to take part, creating an exciting buzz of discovery. This series was one of the most-loved by festival audiences, a real celebration of STEM.

TechFest is grateful to Chevron for their support of the Eureka series as well as BP and Shell, their joint principal festival sponsors, and all the many other organisations that have supported this much-loved festival for the past 24 years.

As well as being a photographer, I was a teacher of 38 years' experience before retiring in 2014. Throughout my teaching career, some of my best memories were of young people engaging in practical science activities and experiencing a sense of anticipation and wonder at the outcomes of their experiments. In the image opposite, taken during one of the Eureka sessions, I wanted to capture that sense of engagement and anticipation.

This session was entitled Chemical Wizardry where the children explored the properties of different substances and how they can be changed as if by magic. They began to learn about the physical and chemical characteristics of substances.

Sarah Chew, Managing Director of Techfest, says: *"It is with fond memories that I look back at this photograph which captured beautifully the concentration and pleasure these children had from learning about science.*

The children are making their preparations to create Elephant's Toothpaste, a fast and dramatic foamy chemical reaction caused by the degradation of hydrogen peroxide. The children have harnessed the power of yeast, a microorganism, to help with the reaction. Hydrogen peroxide is used in bleaches, dyes and cleaning products in our homes but is also a waste product created in our own bodies. It is very reactive and very toxic, so our bodies make it safe by using an enzyme (or digester) to break it down.

A careful squeeze of dish soap means the yeast solution is ready for action. When the hydrogen peroxide is added with a cool nerve and a steady hand, the enzyme in yeast, called catalase, breaks the molecule apart, making water and oxygen in a fast and foamy eruption that gives out lots of heat.

Why is it called Elephant's Toothpaste? It looks like an elephant has trod on a giant tube of toothpaste.

I am so very grateful to be part of this fantastic organisation and it is a privilege to meet the next generation and be part of their learning journey."

Waiting for a Reaction, TechFest

Joan Eardley's Catterline

Discovering The Artist's 'Voice'

David Johnston is a widely-exhibited landscape artist based in the North East of Scotland who has, in recent years, found inspiration in the works of Joan Eardley and the village of Catterline.

David has lectured on the subject, painted the Catterline environment in his own distinctive way and has begun to offer painting courses in the village. Here he reflects on Joan Eardley as a towering figure in the art world and Catterline as a special place for artists to immerse themselves -

"Catterline's origins go back to the Stone Age and the village has been inhabited continuously since the twelfth century. Whether approached from the north or south, the visitor's first impression is of the row of tiny white cottages clinging to the clifftop. Even on a first visit, the place seems strangely familiar through its associations with the work of Joan Eardley.

Catterline provided the inspiration for Joan's finest work. She spent more than a decade there - the landscapes and seascapes in and around the village provided her with all her main themes. And it was there too that she discovered her own distinctive 'voice' as an artist.

Her work speaks to us of the seasons: of ploughed fields in spring, the shimmering heat across the land at hairst time, the intricate freedom of wild flowers in late summer hedgerows and the cold of a winter dawn when the sea is all white in the bay.

Joan Eardley's reputation as a major force in twentieth century British art is justified precisely because her work taps into these universal themes: Man's links with the past, the endless cycle of the seasons and the elemental forces of nature.

Today's visitor will find Catterline much as it was in the early 1950s when Joan first visited the place: it remains a simple settlement which speaks of universal things. I, for one, am glad it hasn't become artificially picturesque for it retains a slightly abandoned, haphazard feel. Cars are still parked on the clifftop side by side with sheds and woodpiles, bikes and barbeques and bits for boats ... and flower barrels still decorate the simple white cottages of South Row.

Whether you come in the sultry heat of a summer's afternoon when the sky is dark out to sea and heavy with thunder, or on a mellow misty evening in October, in the depth of a winter's day or best of all, perhaps, in late spring when the sea is calm and the haar steals over the cliffs to soften the edges of the landscape, Catterline is a place for all seasons and never disappoints."

The image opposite represents Joan Eardley's love of painting winter seas at Catterline. Her biographer Cordelia Oliver described her battle with the elements as stimulating and feeding Joan's creative urge.

Catterline Bay in Winter

Uras Skyline

The River Dee beyond Braemar

The Grit And The Glint

Scotland's National Theatre

The National Theatre of Scotland has built up an international reputation for its pioneering approach to participatory arts projects. The trailblazing model sees teams of professional theatre artists working in towns and cities across Scotland for months at a time to co-create pieces of theatre that leave a longstanding impact on the communities involved.

When Aberdeen was chosen as a location, the theme of the project was Granite: the stone from which the city was built, upon which the city's global reputation has grown and the characteristics of which the people of North East Scotland are widely held to personify – a distinctive character of resilience, grit and robustness.

In the course of producing Granite, the team researched stories that described local people's personal relationships with their home city. Associate Director Simon Sharkey chose a team of world-class creative artists to work with some of the city's leading creative groups who contributed ideas and performing talent. The result was a triumph of bringing Scotland's National Theatre together with community arts.

Simon recalls: *"We were invited to tell the story of Aberdeen and, in particular, the story of the Diaspora that left and arrived in the city throughout the ages. It was a challenge we couldn't refuse and so we set about getting to know The Silver City.*

We embedded artists throughout the city of Aberdeen and began to involve communities that have shaped it throughout its history. What we found was phenomenal. Aberdeen has a long history of sons and daughters who have helped to shape the world.

I was delighted to hear the stories of thousands of people who travelled the world with their skills, their poetry and their sense of purpose.

The image opposite is from the final scene in Granite where the Bisset family returns, exhausted from their adventure to Russia where they had travelled to teach the cutting of granite. It depicts the moment of total collapse of hope and the devastation that giving in brings.

As a result, the community of Aberdeen steps in to offer help. The form of that help is a metaphor, a call to dig deep into the elements that have shaped the North East character.

The family is offered a stone - Granite. The Grit and the Glint. The whole city comes out and shares that grit and glint with them and they rise from their position of despair to one of total triumph. They walk offstage to a bright new dawn of possibility.

This, for me, is the character of Aberdeen. From farming to fishing, through granite production, shipbuilding, education and oil, the sense of place and belonging are palpable. The ability to seize opportunity runs through the people like the mica sparkle that runs through the stone."

The National Theatre of Scotland's "Granite"

Bringing Food To The Table

The Farming Industry

Cllr. Bill Howatson is a former Provost of Aberdeenshire and has served as a local councillor since 1999. As an award-winning journalist, he worked on the Press and Journal in Aberdeen where he was Agricultural Editor from 1984 to 1996 -

"Farming and the land have intrigued and fascinated me all of my life. As a young lad growing up in Dumfriesshire, I learned the basic skills of agriculture – stooking grain sheaves, milking cows, gathering potatoes, hoeing turnips, feeding pigs – from my father.

As a journalist with the Press and Journal, I was privileged to report on the farming industry looking at it with a fresh detachment; chronicling the good times and the bad; delving into the politics of a rapidly changing industry and watching it rise and fall in public perception depending on the latest animal welfare scare and farm subsidies.

And all the time measuring the growing disconnect between an increasingly urban world and the purpose and function of the farm and the farmer in bringing food to the table in the 20th and 21st centuries. In that regard, Aberdeenshire is arguably the last bastion in Scotland where threads of that connection still exist.

Agriculture in Aberdeenshire is on the cusp of radical change due to decreasing farmer numbers, a reduction in the number of medium-sized holdings, over-capacity in the vital red meat sector and a loss of milk producers over the last 15 years.

But the farming industry in Aberdeenshire has an innate sense of resilience, entrepreneurial flair, a strong co-operative presence, and an ambitious and innovative food and drink sector.

I have never looked at farming and the land in a sentimental way. They have given me a sense of place, an appreciation of the vicissitudes of life on the land, and the recognition that the landward areas are not Arcadian wonders but places of work and production.

Over the years, some writers have created a bucolic vision of the land. Others have refreshingly told the truth. David Kerr Cameron, in Willie Gavin, Crofter Man, stood up to the mark, while decades before him, John R Allan's North-East Lowlands of Scotland offered an invaluable study of the characteristics that shaped and defined this part of Scotland.

But in terms of separating sentiment and reality, Lewis Grassic Gibbon made an unparalleled and timeless contribution in his essay on the land. "That is the Land out there, under the sleet, churned and pelted there in the dark, the long rigs upturning their clayey faces to the spear-onset of the sleet.

"Those folk in the byre whose lantern light is a glimmer through the sleet as they muck and tend the kye, and milk the milk into the tin pails, in curling froth – they are The Land in as great a measure."

The Hairst

Living In Fittie

Defining An Artist

Joyce W Cairns RSA,RSW,Hon.RBA,MA(RCA) is an artist of international reputation. Much of her inspiration has come from the village of Fittie in Aberdeen where she has lived for a large part of her life -

"I moved to Footdee, otherwise known as Fittie, the former fishing village at the mouth of Aberdeen Harbour in August 1979.

Despite my thirty three years in the house, it was always known as Jimmy Leiper's. Jimmy ran a shop in what became my dining room. He would sell fishing bait with one hand and then cut up cheese with the other.

It was the house of my dreams, unspoiled by insensitive modernisation. My studio on the top of the house had a fabulous view out to the North Pier. There was a constant stream of oil boats, occasional Naval destroyers and, in summer, the Royal Yacht Britannia coming into the harbour.

Fittie defined me as an artist and it continues to be the catalyst for many of my works. From this base of village, shed, sea, boats, piers and harbour, I reach out to portray the human condition through family memories and relevant artefacts intermingled with the effects of various wars.

Fittie consists of around a hundred buildings of all shapes and sizes built around squares with drying greens and a range of eccentric and personalised sheds including a few original black tarred ones. These housed the nets for drying and bait lines but are now home to the washing machine and freezer.

In 1979, there were few incomers, no benches or pot plants outside the houses and absolutely no washing hung out on a Sunday. The only activities were services in the Mission Hall in the centre of the village and the brethren singing unaccompanied in the Gospel Hall next to my house.

In 1990, I was able to rent the Gospel Hall. This became my studio until 2014. Under the pulpit was a large, deep, zinc bath with a cold tap and wooden steps which was accessed by trap doors. According to older residents, people used to be baptised wearing white gowns and dunked under the water.

Over the years, there have been many changes. The wonderful old characters who twitched their curtains when I moved into the village are long gone.

There was an old lady who used to hand me sea trout hidden under her pinny which she had pinched from the Harbour Board's salmon nets. Old 'Willum' Baxter from North Square would give me scallop shells with pictures of roses pasted on the underside.

It used to be "Aye you're nae fae here, you'll be fae the toon" to an outsider even if only born a few streets away from the village.

It is different now as the majority in the village are outsiders and that has hugely enriched the community, many of whom work hard not only to protect and preserve Fittie but are also initiating schemes which will continue to benefit locals and " fae the toon" in future."

Fittie

Watching The River Flow

The Water of Feugh

The Water of Feugh is the largest tributary of the River Dee. Its source is in the Forest of Birse and it merges with the Dee across from the Banchory Lodge Hotel.

The confluence is the favourite place of Aberdeen businessman Sir Ian Wood, former chairman of the Wood Group which has had a major role to play in the North Sea oil industry. The Group has grown from a modestly-sized company operating principally in a local market to become a global corporation with operations in over 50 countries.

Sir Ian explains why this view is so meaningful to him -

"The image of the River Feugh looks superb, particularly with the changing tree colours. Among the reasons I really love it is that I have visited the Banchory Lodge Hotel on many occasions over the last 50 years, originally with my mother, father and sisters, then with my own family, and now with grandchildren.

It's a truly beautiful spot, very much changing with the seasons, but the confluence of the Feugh flowing into the Dee, which can range from being quiet and peaceful to a raging torrent, commands interest and attention with something always happening, whether its salmon jumping or heron fishing, or the constantly changing water flow. It is just one of many beautiful scenes in the North East of Scotland, but it's the constant movement and activity that I find particularly attractive.

The night I finished my University final exams, I went out to the Bridge of Feugh with a number of my classmates and we sat on the island just above the bridge for probably an hour and a half. It was midnight, but the reassuring sound of the constant flowing water, the wind in the trees, and the peace and still of the night was very relaxing and reassuring at a time of significant change in my life.

So I guess it's a mix of the beauty and the many memories that makes it special for me."

Just beyond the Bridge of Feugh is a water cascade where salmon leap as they make their way upriver during the spawning season. This is the time when salmon have travelled from the North Sea to make their way to the upper reaches of the river where they spawn on gravel beds.

The best sightings from the viewing platform at the bridge are from September to November in the winter run and in February and March for the spring run. It is a dramatic sight as salmon try to propel themselves up through the waterfall, often against a raging spate in the opposite direction.

To photograph autumn colours at their most vibrant, it is important to exploit a window of opportunity between a hard frost and a period of strong winds. The Dee Valley is a rich source of glorious autumn images every October.

The Water of Feugh at Banchory

Songs Of The Fishing

Isla St. Clair

The career of Isla St Clair has spanned more than five decades. As a broadcaster and folksinger, she has performed nationally in many popular radio and and television light entertainment shows as well as touring in concert throughout the world. Brought up in Scotland's North East she remains one of Britain's foremost traditional singers -

"The world of traditional seafaring songs has been considerably enriched by the contribution made by local bards of Aberdeenshire and those who have been inspired by this rugged coastline and its peoples. Versions of these songs are to be found in various parts of the world having been transported by nostalgic émigrés and travellers.

However, a considerable number of songs were lost (perhaps never conceived) as a result of the great religious conversions of the 19th century which brought hymns with powerful seafaring images to the area. Great favourites were those from the collection of the American evangelists Sankey and Moody. These hymns became so popular that they were sung with much enthusiasm in the local alehouses, to the horror of their composers. Ironically, a good number of traditional favourites of the same time would have pled for temperance!

Some of the traditional songs that have survived to the present day have, with the aid of modern technology, gained a considerable and appreciative worldwide audience, occasionally topping the popular charts. For example, a whaling song, 'Farewell Tae Tarwathie', written by George Scroggie, a native of New Deer, around eighteen hundred and fifty, was a worldwide hit for American songstress Judy Collins more than a century later. She was accompanied by the exquisite singing of humpback whales.

The legendary composer and folk singer Ewan MacColl was inspired by the North East herring fishing trade to write his award-winning radio ballad programme 'Singing the Fishing'. His songs such as 'Shoals Of Herring' and 'The Fishgutter's Song' capture the boom times of the herring trade and clearly describe the harsh lives of the fisherfolk from this part of Scotland.

My mother, Georzetta ('Zetta) Sinclair, born in nineteen hundred and twenty, was the youngest child in a North East fishing family, experiencing first-hand the extraordinary daily struggles in harsh weather conditions that her folk had to contend with. Their hopes, fears and strength of character to survive in this most dangerous of trades, the fishing, were remarkable and yet these people still retained a sense of tenderness and humour shared generously amongst those most loved.

Her lullabye 'Lullin The Littlun' and song about a fishing disaster 'The Lifeboat' along with songs describing her mother's life are good reflections of 'Zetta's childhood experiences and, I feel, important social records, especially as the century progressed and the fishing industry was to go into irreversible decline.

It is with great pride and joy that since my childhood, I have been able to bring my mother's songs, as well as many other traditional songs from Scotland's North East fishing communities to audiences throughout the world, casting some light on my remarkable ancestors."

Crovie, Banffshire Coast

A Traditional Spectacle

Highland Games

Jim Brown MBE is Past President of the Scottish Highland Games Association. Jim reflects on the special place that Highland Games continue to have on the culture of the North East of Scotland -

"Highland Games are the special ambassadors of our Aberdeenshire rural events They stand open-armed and welcome visitors and locals, rich and poor, old and young to their unique interpretation of a tradition that had its first stirrings at Braemar some 900 years ago.

Unlike many traditions, Highland Games are a living reality rather than an ancient memory. They have survived rebellions and reformations and spanned changing ways of life. This deeply-ingrained and much-loved tradition continues to flourish, influencing sports and culture all over the world. Over the centuries, there have been laws and acts to ban such gatherings but the deep roots of tradition have held firm and international Highland Games have never been stronger.

Aberdeenshire and the North East of Scotland is the home of some of the finest and the oldest. From the rugged braes of Tomintoul to the smooth turf of Hazlehead in the city of Aberdeen, from the royal formality of Braemar to the complete informality of Drumtochty, from the youthful history of Cornhill to the the ancient story of The Lonach, from the grandeur of Gordon Castle to the playing fields of Stonehaven and Oldmeldrum, from the Deeside gems of Aboyne and Ballater to the Speyside malts of Dufftown, Aberlour and Grantown – all so different but with a shared spirit of friendship and fair competition.

The magical atmosphere at our games is created by a unique combination of wonderful locations, the local character of the committees and the continuous performances of Highland heavy athletes, the unyielding tug o' war teams, the swift track runners, the colourful vibrancy of the dancers, the unforgettable sound of massed pipe bands, the haunting pibrochs of solo pipers and the backdrop of lively stalls and side shows. A truly safe and welcoming family gathering where international professional performers uniquely share an arena with impromptu children's events.

No visit to our beloved Aberdeenshire is complete without the Highland Games Experience"

As a photographer, Highland Games arenas offer a multitude of opportunities. My friend Jim Brown has often allowed me access to the arena at Drumtochty near Auchenblae which has one of the most idyllic settings that I have seen anywhere in Scotland. The image opposite is of former World Champion Alistair Gunn of Halkirk, in full swing, throwing the hammer at the Drumtochty Highland Games. Athletes, dancers, pipers, drummers, colour, tradition; it is all there, with much of the activity happening simultaneously, creating a unique atmosphere.

The Braemar Gathering on Royal Deeside takes place on the first Saturday of September each year when several members of the Royal Family are usually in attendance, including the Patron, Her Majesty the Queen.

Drumtochty Highland Games

Harley Headlamps, Grampian Transport Museum, Alford

Fred's Sheds (Ship's Painter), Fraserburgh Harbour

A Distinguished Fiddle Tradition

Paul Anderson

Paul Anderson from Tarland is one of the most respected exponents of the Scots fiddle tradition in Scotland today. Paul explains the fiddle's place in North East musical culture -

"Scotland has a very long and distinguished fiddle tradition and one of its most distinctive regional styles is that found in the North East counties of Moray, Angus and my own native Aberdeenshire.

Some of Scotland's most important traditional fiddle players and composers came from the North East of Scotland, underlining the region's importance in the development of the fiddle player's art.

Figures like William Marshall of Fochabers whom the fiddle-playing bard Robert Burns so admired, Hector MacAndrew of Fyvie, Bill Hardie of Aberdeen, James Scott Skinner the "Strathspey King" of Banchory, and his tutor Peter Milne the "Tarland Minstrel" are amongst Scotland's most revered and iconic traditional musicians and it's partly down to their legacy that there is an unbroken tradition of fiddle playing in the North East of Scotland from the distant past to the present day.

The other key reason for the survival and current popularity of traditional fiddle music is the work of groups such as the Banchory Strathspey and Reel Society, the Garioch Fiddlers, the Fochabers Fiddlers and the Aberdeen Strathspey and Reel Society to name but a few. Groups like these kept the musical flame alive when there was little interest from the media and the tradition seemed like it might die out. They've encouraged thousands of people to enjoy, appreciate and indeed perform this priceless cultural heirloom and all without any financial assistance.

My own love affair with the instrument started upon finding an old fiddle under the spare bed at my grandparents' house at the Mains of Kincraigie near Tarland when I was about five years of age. I took to the fiddle with enthusiasm and it would probably have been around this time that I first really noticed the handsome granite memorial stone to Tarland's most famous son, Peter Milne, and became conscious of there being a long tradition of fiddle playing on my own doorstep; the "fiddlers o' Tarland" performed for Queen Victoria and Prince Albert when they first visited Deeside in 1848.

Tomnaverie Stone Circle sits in the heart of the Howe o' Cromar and it has always been a place I've loved to spend time at and quite a few of my compositions were written there. Below the sacred hill with its enigmatic standing stones lies the whole of the Howe, the fields my family farmed, the church of St Moluag's which my great, great, great grandfather helped to build, the Muir o' Gellan where the young Peter Milne worked as a cattle herd and the Mains of Kincraigie where I first discovered the old French fiddle and where I now live with my family.

Lochnagar and Morven stand sentinel and timeless over the land and it's impossible not to be inspired by the beauty and the the threads which link the past with the present."

Tomnaverie Stone Circle, Tarland

The March Of The Lonach Highlanders

A Donside Tradition

Jennifer Stewart is the secretary and chief executive of the Lonach Highland and Friendly Society. The daughter of a Lonach Highlander, Jennifer was elected to the role of secretary and chief executive in 2009, becoming the first female to hold the position in the society's history -

"In the early morning of the fourth Saturday of every August, the Aberdeenshire valley of Strathdon rouses in preparation for the day ahead. By 7.30am the village of Bellabeg is a hive of activity as crowds mingle while plaids are folded, tunics get straightened, pipes are tuned and a horse is hitched to a cart.

At 8am, with crowds lining the road, the skirl of the pipes and beat of the drums strike up and lead a body of around 170 men on a six-mile march that retraces the footsteps of their forefathers. Dressed in full highland attire and shouldering eight-foot long pikes or carrying Lochaber axes, the Lonach Highlanders are a stunning sight and sound as they march through some of Scotland's most beautiful scenery.

Following the marchers and adding to that sight and sound is the Lonach horse and cart. In days gone by, as the men marched over rough hill roads the cart would have carried the pikes and axes when they became too heavy to carry. Today, the horse and cart continue that tradition, but some say the potential cargo may be different!

As the march winds its way through picturesque Strathdon, it halts at six local properties that are the homes of notable local figures or landowners. It's a ritual that stretches back to the first Lonach Highland Gathering and Games held in 1832. At each stop, the highlanders receive a dram of whisky, with which they toast the health of the property's owner, the Lonach Highland and Friendly Society and the local area with the cry of Ho Ho Lonach, which echoes round the valley.

The Lonach Highlanders are believed to be the largest body of non-military men to carry ceremonial weapons in Britain and at 1pm their arrival at the Lonach Highland Gathering and Games is greeted with great cheers and applause. With kilts swinging, row upon row of pikes glistening in the sunshine and the sound of pipe bands reverberating round the arena, it is a stunning spectacle that invokes many emotions.

The event was founded to provide an occasion for members of the Lonach Highland and Friendly Society to come together to commemorate the society's 1823 inception. Attracting up to 10,000 visitors each year, it is one of Scotland's oldest and most iconic highland games. Featuring a full programme of traditional highland events, it celebrates and helps to preserve the history, heritage and culture of the Lonach area."

The Lonach March, Strathdon

An Architect's Vision

Union Square

Union Square is the second largest city centre shopping development in Scotland. It opened in October 2009 and, over two floors, contains a wide variety of modern retail units, a diverse range of restaurants and a cinema. Visually, it is exciting and contemporary.

Ross Fletcher of Building Design Partnership was the architect of Union Square. The design was the culmination of meetings and consultations with many stakeholders. As a result of this collaborative dialogue, BDP produced a visionary and innovative design which is both aesthetic and functional, visually enhancing the whole area around Guild Street.

Here, Ross describes the creative process -

"For an architect, the challenge of imagining and creating Union Square was special, the opportunity to graft on a new piece to the beautiful, dynamic and historic Aberdeen City Centre.

The Shopping Centre knits itself into the city, nestling amongst the harbour with its imposing rig supply vessels, the buzz of the train station and bus station, a short jaunt down from Union Street itself.

A few episodes of 'Grand Designs' gives useful insight into what a big difference 'design' makes to people's lives, the trick always being to talk to people, understand their needs, understand what is really important, what is the real challenge and then, apply thinking caps, add an 'x-factor' idea and imagine a building that delights and surprises and does much more than just join the dots.

A key element in integrating into the urban fabric of Aberdeen was the creation of a new civic square in front of the existing railway station. This space acts as a hub, collecting the various people-routes through the site whilst providing a focal point for the historic pedestrian streets and closes linking the Green to Union Street. This new space becomes the gateway to Aberdeen for those approaching by rail, bus or sea.

Today the 'shopping mall' has become a big part of people's lives. Whilst on the one hand generally experiencing a mixed press, sometimes as the villain of the peace usurping well-loved and age-worn local shops and town centre, on the other hand it has become a much relied upon reference point for people week to week.

A visit to your favourite centre is now a key leisure, family and social activity. The shape of work life, family time and leisure time is changing - more opportunities, more time pressures, many more ways to communicate, many more ways to visit 'virtual' places, many different ways to make a purchase without face to face connection.

Union Square provides an answer to often unspoken needs, a lively and vibrant collection of businesses, shops, leisure, information, transport options. A place providing community, a place for people, a new place for Aberdeen."

Late Night Shopping at Union Square

Aberdeenshire Distilled

The Whisky Industry

Aberdeenshire plays host to eight whisky distilleries:- Ardmore, Fettercairn, Glendronach, Glengarioch, Glenglassaugh, Knockdhu, Macduff and Royal Lochnagar. The history of each, in combination with the craft traditions handed down from generation to generation and influenced by the distilleries' locations, combine to produce the unique character of the malt whisky made by each distillery.

Ardmore Distillery stands deep in rural Aberdeenshire near Kennethmont. It is the malt at the heart of the Teacher's blends. Highland Cream was the first whisky to use a stopper cork, introduced in 1913. The firm advertised under the slogan "Bury the Corkscrew".

Fettercairn Distillery is in the fertile Mearns region of South Aberdeenshire, Sunset Song country. Established by Sir Alexander Ramsay, the laird of Fasque, in 1824, it was sold in 1830 to Sir John Gladstone, father of Prime Minister William Ewart Gladstone. The distillery is now owned by Whyte & Mackay Ltd.

Glendronach Distillery, situated at Forgue, near Huntly, was built in 1825 by a group of local farmers and businessmen led by James Allardice. Allardice so impressed the local laird, the Duke of Gordon, that he was introduced by the Duke to London Society where he established a reputation for his "Guid Glendronach."

Glengarioch Distillery, built in 1797, is located at Oldmeldrum. On one occasion, the distillery employed a famous water diviner, Neil Murchie, known as the "Water Mannie o' Foggieloan" who spoke in broad Doric, making it almost impossible for the translator who was trying to interpret for a Japanese representative of Suntory.

Royal Lochnagar Distillery is named after the mountain that rises up behind the distillery and Balmoral Castle, Scottish home of the Royal Family. Queen Victoria and Prince Albert who initially leased, then bought and rebuilt Balmoral Castle were invited to tour the distillery in 1848 and, after being given a dram, awarded a Royal Warrant.

The Knockdhu Distillery, established in 1894, nestles quietly in the shadow of the mysterious Black Hill in the Scottish Highlands. A traditional, enchanting distillery where a curiously modern Single Malt named anCnoc, meaning simply 'the hill', is crafted.

Macduff is a modern distillery built primarily to supply malt whisky for blending. Only a small amount is bottled, under the name of The Deveron.

Glenglassaugh Distillery, situated on the Moray Firth coast of Aberdeenshire, is home to a spirit that is still handcrafted by a small, highly-skilled team. After many years out of production, the restored distillery was reopened in 2008.

Whisky writer Charles MacLean, described by The Times as "Scotland's leading whisky expert", reflects on the whisky industry in Aberdeenshire -

"Known in the trade as "East Highland Malts", the whiskies of Aberdeenshire are wonderfully diverse in flavour. Ardmore is smoky, Glenglassaugh slightly salty, anCnoc and The Deveron are light and fruity. GlenDronach is magnificently rich; Glen Garioch often gingery, Fettercairn nutty. The noble Royal Lochnagar, bosky and complex. All are hugely rewarding."

The Spirit Still, Glenglassaugh Distillery

For The Common Good

King Robert the Bruce

The image opposite is of Marischal College towering above a statue of Robert the Bruce, King of Scots, holding aloft the Royal Charter that he gave to Aberdeen.in exchange for its help in the first Scottish War of Independence.

Neil McLennan, Past President of the Scottish Association of Teachers of History and presently Senior Lecturer and Director of Leadership Programmes at Aberdeen University explains the significance of these two landmarks in the city's history -

"1486 is not usually associated with Robert the Bruce. Many key dates resonate with the King of Scots. 1306, his seizing of the throne; less than a decade later, victory at Bannockburn ensured that 1314 is etched in the minds of many; meanwhile, 1313 saw him grant his first Royal Charter to Aberdeen.

So why 1486? Well, it is the number of votes cast for the statue in this picture. It took four years for sculptor Alan Beattie Herriot to make the 18 feet 4 inches representation of the mediaeval King of Scots. In a nice 'pay it back' moment, the £120,000 it cost to build was taken from the Common Good Fund that Bruce set up in in 1319.

Earlier Royal Charters had been granted to Aberdeen by William the Lion and David I; however, Bruce granted six charters in recognition of the support of the city. They are viewed as influential in the growth of the city, not least the forming of the Common Good Fund in 1319. Since then, the fund has supported Aberdeen folk in education, civic projects, healthcare support and cultural enterprises.

Another magnificent enterprise stands behind the horsebacked Bruce holding aloft the Royal Charter. The statue is placed in front of the second largest granite structure in the world.

In 1593, Marischal College opened. Unlike its Kings College neighbour in Old Aberdeen, this university was to serve the new town and was the second post-reformation university. Founded by George Keith, fourth Earl Marischal, it would eventually merge with Bishop Elphinstone's 1495 founded university in 1860, forming the modern day University of Aberdeen.

The buildings of Marischal College were not always the grand ones that you see today. Construction on the current building began in the 1830s with the pinnacle façade finished in 1906. Today this awe-inspiring granite building (second only in size to Madrid's El Escorial) and its 400 feet long and 80 feet high façade is visited and has been photographed by many from tourists to top photographers like Andy Hall.

Whilst only 1,486 voted, one can almost guarantee that many more have visited the statue and photographed it and the magnificent building that it sits in front of. Moreover, many, many more have benefited from both Bruce's Fund and the education provided by both the fund and, of course, the city's ancient university."

By coincidence, Neil spent several years working out of Marischal College as a senior education officer. Furthermore, Neil's family tree reveals relatives as descendants of Bruce.

King Robert the Bruce Statue and Marischal College

Cruden Bay Golf Club and Slains Castle

Balmedie Beach

Social History In Song

Bothy Ballads

Bothy Ballads were songs that were sung by farmworkers in Scotland during the nineteenth and early twentieth centuries. Aberdeenshire was a particularly rich source; the Greig-Duncan Folk Song Collection comprised eight volumes!

Bothies were farm outbuildings where unmarried labourers would sleep after a long day in the fields. In the evenings, they would entertain themselves by singing songs. Humorous stories would be exchanged between the workers to distract themselves from the often harsh conditions that they had been working in during the day.

Farming provided work for thousands of North East folk. Landowners leased their land in lots to farmers for agreed terms who, in turn, employed labourers for the seasonal work. At the bigger farms, the farmers employed a grieve as a general manager. Next in line was the ploughman, the most respected and best paid of the workers, the "orra man" or cattleman and, after him, the general labourers and the "orra loon", a young jack of all trades.

Workers were hired or "fee'd" for a six month period at the local Feein' Markets held in towns and villages a week or so before the beginning of the terms: Whitsunday (May) and Martinmas (November). Women, too, were appointed for set terms usually to work in the kitchens, cooking for the farmer's family and the "bothy loons." These "kitchie deems" were kept hard at work under the watchful eye of the farmer's wife.

Home for the unmarried worker was a chaumer, or bothy, but conditions, especially during the 19th century, were often inferior to the byres and stables which housed the cattle and Clydesdale horses which were the valuable assets of the farmer. The labourers were expendable unless you were a skilled horseman and therefore not to be taken for granted. Horsemen were responsible for a pair of horses and promotion came with the position of the pair - Third, Second, First Billie.

It was in bothies like this that Bothy Ballads originated, otherwise known as "Cornkisters" where the audience and singers kept time to the music with their heels whilst sitting on chests filled with corn to feed the horses. They grew from the experiences of the men and women working in and around the farms of the 19th and 20th centuries. They were set largely to existing pipe and fiddle tunes.

Bothy Ballads are a rich source of social history of rural farming life when horse-drawn ploughs were at the heart of the agriculture industry in Aberdeenshire.

The tradition is kept alive today by singers who compete for cups and trophies at farm shows and gatherings. Shona Donaldson, originally from Huntly, became the first female winner of the Bothy Ballads Champion of Champions in February 2016.

Shona Donaldson

Turriff Showtime

For A'body

The Turriff Show is the largest two day agricultural show in Scotland. It is held every year on the Sunday and Monday before the first Tuesday in August.

Thousands of people descend on the Aberdeenshire town to see the cream of Scotland's livestock, the latest in agricultural machinery and an imaginative range of stalls and entertainment. It is a place of business and of fun.

Helen Paterson, Secretary of the Turriff Show describes the background -

"The first Turriff Show was held in 1864 and was an agricultural meeting and general show of livestock, implements of husbandry and dairy produce held at what was called the Market Stance. It then moved to its present day show field at The Haughs in 1924 when the ring was reported to be one of the most spacious and level in the country.

In 2008, the Turriff Show won the Northern Lights Tourism Award and in 2013 the Farmers Guardian Award for the best show in the UK.

There is always a fantastic array of prize-winning cattle, sheep, horses, ponies, goats and small animals as well as many lines of impressive farm machinery with over 250 quality outdoor trade stands selling a wide range of goods as well as a Food Fayre marquee, an indoor shopping mall, an exhibition marquee and an arts and crafts marquee. One of the largest marquees displays home-based crafts, flowers, fruit and vegetables.

Livestock and trade-stand exhibitors and judges attend from the length and breadth of the UK and also from abroad. Over the years, many national Cattle and Sheep Shows have been hosted by the Turriff Show.

The exciting ringside programme varies from year to year with motorcycle displays, jousting on horseback and the favourites of horse jumping, sulky trotting and the Sunday evening finale of the Vintage Vehicle Parade.

One of the most memorable highlights of the Turriff Show was in 2014, the 150th Anniversary, when we were very honoured and privileged to have Her Majesty The Queen attend on the Monday. She visited various parts of the show and was introduced to a variety of officials, some of whom were lucky enough to have lunch with her. Before departing, Her Majesty enjoyed various events in the ring and presented the Supreme Overall Champion Trophy.

With 30,000 visitors to the show every year, it is seen as a meeting place and is one of the main shop windows in Scotland with something for everyone, no matter what their age."

The image opposite is a Scottish Blackface sheep. One of the aspects that I really enjoy about the Turriff Show is that all the exhibited animals are in pristine condition after hours of preparation. The pictured Scottish Blackface is a good example of this. Despite being in the open-air, it looks like it is sitting for a portrait in a photographer's studio!

Scottish Blackface, Turriff Show

Jolomo's Inspiration

The Aberdeenshire Coast

Dr. John Lowrie Morrison OBE, better-known in the art world by his sobriquet of Jolomo, has gained international recognition for his vibrant and colourful works that are instantly recognisable. He explains what the North East coastline means to him -

"The Aberdeenshire coast has been a great inspiration for me for many years since seeing Joan Eardley's Memorial Exhibition in Kelvingrove Art Galleries in 1963. Her wonderfully evocative and expressive paintings of Catterline have resonated with me ever since, and have introduced me to the Aberdeenshire coast.

Most people associate me with painting the Scottish west coast .. particularly lighthouses and crofts. Croftscapes .. as I call them .. are an intrinsic part of my 'Oeuvre' and have been for 50 years.

However, although I am mainly drawn towards the ever-changing light of the west coast, I have often painted the coast of Aberdeenshire which also has a stunning light that is sometimes quite different from the west light.

The coastline of west and east are completely different. The west, being bashed by the North Atlantic, has thousands of deep fjord-type sea lochs .. with many towns and villages in safe parts at the head of lochs. The east, particularly Aberdeenshire, does not have this type of coast and is much more open and therefore much more open to the elements .. with towns and villages 'snuck' under cliffs like Crovie, Pennan and part of Gardenstown.

I love this idea of living among the elements … the sea ready to engulf the houses .. which I have seen in these villages .. massive waves crashing over the sea-facing gables of dozens of Aberdeenshire hamlets. Nerves of steel are required to live here I think!

What is also inspiring and wonderful though, is the difference sometimes in the light between the Aberdeenshire coast and the Argyllshire coast. The sun obviously being in different places on the Scottish mainland .. moving from east to west .. creates different light sources and depths of colour which I find extremely interesting.

And the clarity and intensity of light on both coasts is quite fantastic with the sea being a big element of that clarity and intensity … with the light being reflected back by the vast waters of the Atlantic and the North Sea. The land itself also reflects back the light … especially the coastal rock which I believe affects reflected light.

This of course gives a different 'feel' to a place and its landscape .. and the Aberdeenshire coast will continue to be great source of motifs for me .. not only because of its quirky villages 'on the edge' .. but especially with its varied lighthouses .. all of which I've painted many times.

The Aberdeenshire coast is a fabulously interesting and inspiring place for a painter. I can't wait to get back!"

Crashing Waves, Aberdeenshire Coast

Treasure Troves Of Heritage

Aberdeenshire in Trust

Sir Moir Lockhead OBE is the Chairman of the National Trust for Scotland. Sir Moir has strong North East connections through his business interests and having his home near Banchory. He was awarded a Doctorate honoris causa by the University of Aberdeen in 2009 and is well placed to give a first-hand evaluation of the importance of the National Trust for Scotland in Aberdeenshire -

"From its rugged coastline to its rolling hills, Aberdeenshire has some of Scotland's best heritage. It has plenty of natural charms with ancient woodlands, dramatic mountains and world famous rivers that are home to salmon, red squirrels, golden eagles and otters, and a lot more besides. The National Trust for Scotland is lucky to play a crucial part in caring for so much of this landscape at places like Mar Lodge Estate.

The area is Scotland's castle capital – our charity alone cares for five of the area's finest, from the petite and pink Craigievar Castle, to the mediaeval drama of Drum Castle and the grand baronial style of Fyvie Castle. There are grand houses too, with Haddo House and Leith Hall and the immaculate box hedges of Pitmedden Garden. These places are treasure troves of heritage, bringing Aberdeenshire's history to life.

I am lucky enough to live very close to one of Aberdeenshire's most impressive castles. Crathes Castle near Banchory has a history which pre-dates Robert the Bruce by quite some way. But it was he who gifted the land to the Burnard family in 1323, starting the story of the estate which survives today. Legend has it that this was presented with the 'Horn of Leys', a beautifully decorated ivory horn that still hangs in the castle.

The castle itself was built with its narrow stairs and painted ceilings over the course of the 16th century in a traditional 'keep' style. Much of its original design remains, despite its long life and the odd fire. The interiors are a time capsule of the Burnett family's life there over many generations, portraits of whom still hang on the walls.

Outside, the gardens have an international reputation, and a long history. There are 18th century yew hedges and in summer, the borders are full of blazing colour. A dragonfly sculpture is just one of the artworks to enjoy and there are real-life examples buzzing about the ponds around the garden and estate giving a small glimpse of the many wild species that can be found exploring the garden and the woodland walks.

But it is in the Warren Field where we sense the true scale of the history here. A series of post holes dating back 10,000 years could be the world's oldest calendar. It is possible that this is where the concept of time was born - and that's quite a claim for Aberdeenshire."

Crathes Castle Gardens, Banchory

A Vision Realised

BrewDog

In 2007, Aberdeenshire friends James Watt and Martin Dickie were disenchanted by the industrially-brewed, unimaginative and conventional beers that dominated the UK market. They decided the best way to change this undesirable situation was to brew their own. In April 2007, BrewDog was born.

Both only 24 at the time, they leased a building in Fraserburgh, got some daunting bank loans, spent all their money on stainless steel and started making hardcore craft beers.

In the beginning, they brewed tiny batches, filled bottles by hand and sold their beers at local markets and out of the back of their beat up old van. Their biggest mission when they set up BrewDog was to make other people as passionate about great craft beer as they were. This remains the principal aim of the company.

Things started to get crazy for them in 2008. They persuaded the banks to give them money to buy many more tanks and a proper bottling machine. They masterminded the UK's strongest ever beer, Tokyo, and started exporting to Sweden, Japan and America. In its second year, BrewDog became Scotland's largest independent brewery.

To keep up with the incredible demand for their beers, BrewDog launched Equity for Punks. In a ground-breaking first, they offered people the opportunity to buy shares in their company online. Over 1,300 people invested. They grew their business by 200% in the worst recession for generations.

Opening their first craft beer bar in their home town of Aberdeen was a dream come true. The response blew them away. Due to the runaway success of flagship BrewDog Aberdeen, they were able to open bars in Edinburgh, Glasgow and a bar in Camden, London. In true BrewDog style they announced their arrival in the capital by driving down Camden High Street in a tank!

In 2012, BrewDog moved from their cobbled-together brewery in Fraserburgh to a state of the art eco-brewery in Ellon. Since then, they have launched the largest crowdfunding scheme in history - Equity Punks IV - breaking world records in the process.

Through producing a high-quality product, left-field marketing imagination, a highly-motivated and inclusive workforce, an innovative funding model and engaging an almost evangelical following, the BrewDog story, which started in the North East of Scotland with two friends having an idea to improve the beer-drinking experience, has become a success story of global proportions.

James Watt reflects on their success - *"BrewDog was born on the rugged coast of North East Scotland and we're still firmly attached to our roots in the region. Aberdeenshire is where we were born, and where we thrive. It provides ample business opportunity. Our local community has supported us vehemently since Day 1."*

BrewDog Eco-Brewery, Ellon

Moods of Cruden Bay

Fiona Kennedy

Fiona Kennedy OBE DL is a much-loved singer, songwriter, broadcaster and producer of stage shows and television productions. She lives in Aberdeenshire and has a home at Cruden Bay. Fiona is very familiar with this beautiful part of the North East -

"I have always felt that this view of Cruden Bay is one of the most wondrous in the North East of Scotland. It is not known to too many people outside the village itself - and maybe that's a good thing!

In days gone by, a steam train from London would chug all the way to Cruden Bay to its rather majestic hotel on the golf course with elegant passengers on board, eager to enjoy the beautiful game, the views and the fresh air.

Although that splendid hotel is long gone, the village can still boast of ever-changing and spectacular, natural light shows above its curved sandy bay where you can walk and still hardly see a soul.

However, I think local folk like to keep this amazing lunar landscape to themselves and quite right too! I love when we're there to take our dogs to chase the waves, run zigzag along the water's edge and just breathe and sing!

If you're lucky enough to be in Cruden Bay on a clear early evening at twilight, you might see a sky bursting with great swathes of burnt oranges, rich reds and dancing with vibrant blues - Mother Nature at her finest - producing an amazing backdrop to the mysterious ruin that is Slains Castle, Bram Stoker's inspiration for writing 'Dracula'.

Andy Hall's stunning photograph, taken pre-dawn, perfectly captures the glory of the early morning light - the almost Arizona-like red sky with the hauntingly black silhouette of Slains Castle holding its own amongst these dramatic colours.

Then there's the crystal sea and gentle rippling waves in the foreground which I often jump around to stop getting my feet too wet.

However, I wouldn't want you to think that the view Andy waited patiently to capture is always like this! There are many wild, windy and rather bleak, grey days when you would hardly believe the sky capable of such a miraculous transformation. The haar comes in and hangs like a witch's cloak for hours - 'pea soupers!'

But strangely, despite sometimes horrendous weather, the light changes quickly and there is calm before the dawn. You can only look in wonder and relish the view."

Cruden Bay at Sunrise

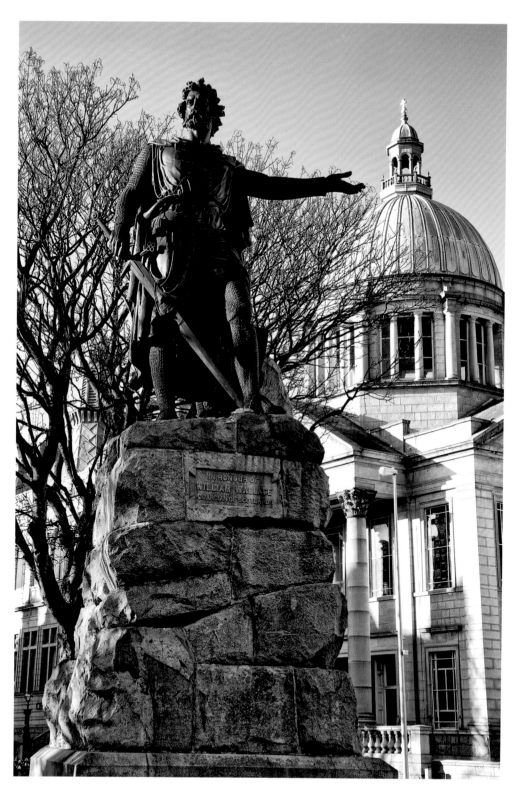

The William Wallace Statue and His Majesty's Theatre

Maggie's, Aberdeen

Valley Of Echoes

Glen Tanar

As well as photography, two of my favourite pastimes are walking and forestry biking. In different seasons, I enjoy visiting Glen Tanar near Aboyne where I can immerse myself in these activities and combine them with experiencing nature in all its forms.

Glen Tanar Estate is part of the Cairngorms National Park. Claire and Michael Bruce own and, along with their staff, manage Glen Tanar Estate. In partnership with the Forestry Commission and Scottish Natural Heritage, they combine modern management methods with traditional knowledge.

Claire describes her experience of living and working in Glen Tanar and the impact of encountering one of the most beautiful parts of Royal Deeside for the first time -

"Glen Tanar has been my home since 1988 when I arrived as a new bride fresh from city life. Frequent trips to the Lake District and the Alps had instilled in me a love of mountains, the outdoors and perpetually changing weather, however Glen Tanar was new and a revelation to me.

In a corner of the North East of Scotland and from my back door at Tillycairn, I uncovered burbling crystal clear burns full of wild watercress, hedgerows framing farmland bursting with rose hips and chattering song birds, and a shy roe deer nibbling at my roses in the garden.

Then, as today, I follow trails down to the River Tanar, along the Firmounth, an ancient highway linking Deeside with the Glens of Angus. I come across carefully constructed drystone dykes, old bridges and Victorian inscribed stones. These were commissioned and placed there by William Cunliffe Brooks in the late nineteenth century. Some are inscribed with historic dates and others with quirky sayings.

Passing by farms and fields of horses, I marvel at buildings designed by the architect George Truefitt and built by an army of stonemasons and craftsmen, now renovated to accommodate more modern amenities.

Walking through the Forest of Glen Tanar, part of the ancient Wood of Caledon, it is breathtaking and I get a strong sense of the people and animals that have shaped this land over centuries. Gnarled and magnificent pine trees have stood the test of time over hundreds of years, while the vast array of native wildlife and indigenous trees are a marvel for those who are lucky enough to witness them.

Standing on the highest point of the most easterly Munro, Mount Keen, I gaze with wonder across windswept heather moorland and the eastern Grampians towards the majestic Lochnagar and into the distant Cairngorms. Glen Tanar was once a relatively isolated glen, home to hardy farmers and loggers.

I stand in admiration looking down the Glen from my vantage point; I see the magnificent landscape tumbling down gently to the Dee Valley ready to welcome the visitors and inhabitants today."

Glentanar Estate, Aboyne

A Living Tongue

Doric

Norman Harper is a journalist, a columnist, an author and a son of the Howe of Alford. He is a highly-respected writer on the subject of North East life in general and, specifically, the indigenous oral dialect which, in many cases, defines the day-to-day character of the area, otherwise known as Doric. It is rich in texture and meaning.

Norman reflects on its value in the everyday lives of the native population -

"This brooding cloudscape, in which you can almost feel the chill of the gale sweeping across bare land and the rain about to thrash everything beneath, impresses everyone who sees it.

But look closer. What really tugs at the heartstrings of the sons and daughters of the North East is not the angry sky but that roofline silhouette; the classic farmhouse of Aberdeenshire, Banffshire and Kincardine for a century and a half.

It is impossible to drive more than a mile in our countryside without seeing at least one, and usually more, of these. They have become iconic. We see them every day to the extent that few of us pay them any heed, but a North East expat anywhere in the world will recognise that outline and begin to feel the pull of home.

They might even lapse into that other icon of their heritage: our speech. The culture in the North East of Scotland is distinctive, and in the vanguard is our dialect, known affectionately as Doric. It is marked by longer vowels and gentler measure than the pacier speech in other parts of Scotland.

Most natives who grew up in the 20th century spoke Doric as their first tongue. Like most of my peers, I did not begin learning English until I went to school, shortly before my fifth birthday. We now flit from one to the other with the ease of anyone who is bilingual.

There is a misconception that Doric is corrupted English. Indeed, some of our own refer to it as slang. They are soon corrected. Doric is one of five dialects of the Scots language. Scots shares roots with English, but is a tongue in its own right. Slang it is not.

To be strictly accurate, there are at least a dozen flavours of Doric, depending on where in the North East you find yourself. We all understand each other, but Aberdonian Doric has different cadences and minor changes in vocabulary to Buchan Doric, which is in turn subtly different from Doric spoken on the Banffshire coast, or down Donside or in Kincardineshire.

Whatever, there are an estimated 250,000 of us who understand it, and nearly as many who speak it fluently. There are even one or two of us who write it.

It is a dialect that speaks of the land and sings of the sea, and we are intensely proud of it."

Fermhoose Silhouette

The Fatherland Of Robert Burns

The Bard's Ancestral Landscape

Internationally acclaimed as Scotland's national poet, Robert Burns was born in a humble cottage in Alloway, Ayrshire, on the 25th of January, 1759. It was, however, the ancient county of Kincardineshire, otherwise known as the Mearns, that was the fatherland of Robert Burns. I have lived in Stonehaven for most of my life and I often walk through the landscape that Burns's ancestors, from his father back to his great, great, grandfather, knew so intimately.

The Burnes (original spelling) family had worked the farms of Bogjurgen and Brawlinmuir before Robert's grandfather settled at Clochnahill, six miles south-west of Stonehaven. He had four sons, George, who died very young, James, Robert and William, the poet's father.

William Burnes' childhood and early life were greatly influenced by the traditions, culture, behaviours and values of the people of the Mearns. As young men, William and his elder brother Robert left Clochnahill together, driven southward by poor farming opportunities, a sense of adventure and the hope of better fortune. William eventually settled with his wife Agnes Broun in Alloway, Ayrshire, where Robert was born in 1759.

The image opposite is taken from the croft ruins of Brawliemuir (derived from Brawlinmuir) where the poet's grandfather, also Robert, was born in 1686. From time to time, I sit among the ruins and reflect that this is the same view that grandfather Robert would have looked out on every day - without, of course, the modern references of contemporary houses and electricity pylons!

I think of the unforgiving and unyielding earth around me that was to be found again in Ayrshire by young Robert. The arduous existence endured by the poet in his early farming days was to be a significant contributory factor to the weakening of his heart and, ultimately, the shortening of his life.

A widely-held view is that Robert's genius came from being a joyous amalgamation of his mother's love of music and song and his father's love of learning. The poet was an avid scholar with a keen intellect and an enquiring mind, largely due to the efforts of his father who ensured that Robert received a diverse and thorough education.

A stone cairn located in a lay-by beside the A90 marks its proximity to Clochnahill, the birthplace of William Burnes. Many of the poet's forebears are buried at Glenbervie Churchyard. The Burns Memorial Garden at the Bridge of Cowie in Stonehaven contains a statue of the poet and is a place to reflect on the area as the cradle of Scotland's National Bard's forefathers.

Robert Burns himself visited the area in 1787 when he described it as *"a rich and cultivated, but still unenclosed country."*

I often reflect that this is the same landscape that had, through previous generations, helped to mould and shape the character and philosophy of Robert Burns.

The Fatherland of Robert Burns

Powering The Nation

St Fergus Gas Terminal

The St. Fergus Gas Terminal is just to the north of the village of St. Fergus on the Aberdeenshire coast, 35 miles north of Aberdeen. It receives natural gas from more than 20 UK and Norwegian North Sea fields via two pipelines and comprises three processing trains with a combined capacity of 2,648 million cubic feet per day. The processing involves the removal of any condensates or liquid hydrocarbons and drying the natural gas for use in homes and workplaces.

There are two other terminals in the vicinity operated by Apache and Shell as well as a compressor station operated by National Grid.

St. Fergus was developed in 1977 by TOTAL E&P UK Limited. The facilities have been upgraded and expanded over the years to cope with the changing mixture of gases and processing requirements from additional fields. It will continue to be an essential hub providing a route for gas into the UK market for decades to come.

In March 2016, the plant was acquired by North Sea Midstream Partners with Teesside based energy and process industry specialist, the px group, becoming responsible for the operations, management and maintenance of the 220 acre site.

All this began back in May 1964 when the UK Continental Shelf Act came into force and seismic exploration on a large scale was launched. The first, though ultimately unsuccessful well, followed later that year.

By 1968, companies lost interest in exploration of the British sector, a result of a ban on gas exports and low prices offered by the only buyer, British Gas.

This completely changed in December 1969, however, when Phillips Petroleum discovered oil at Ekofisk in Norwegian waters in the central North Sea. The same month, Amoco unearthed the Montrose Field about 135 miles east of Aberdeen.

BP discovered the giant Forties Oil Field in October 1970 and the following year, Shell Expro found the huge Brent Oil Field in the northern North Sea, east of Shetland, while the Petronord Group discovered the Frigg Gas Field.

The Piper Oil Field was discovered in 1973 as offshore production became more economical following that year's oil crisis, which caused the world oil price to quadruple. In 1979, the energy crisis led to a further tripling of the price.

Since then, the exploration of the North Sea has been a story of continually pushing back the boundaries of technology. By the 1980s, costs for developing new methods and applications to improve efficiency and safety far exceeded NASA's moon landing budget.

Around 180 people are employed at the St. Fergus Terminal. Some have been recruited locally or moved to the area. They join the many thousands of others attracted to the beautiful North East coast by the oil and gas industry – many of whom have stayed after retirement.

St Fergus Oil and Gas Refinery at Night

The Pursuit Of Truth

The University of Aberdeen

When I enter Old Aberdeen High Street, it is like stepping back in time. Historic residences and university buildings line the cobbled street. The crown of King's College of the University of Aberdeen dominates the skyline.

Professor Sir Ian Diamond is Principal and Vice-Chancellor, an appointment he has held since the 1st of April 2010. He explains the academic, economic and cultural significance of the university in the 21st Century -

"521 years ago our founder, Bishop Elphinstone, set out to create a centre of learning for northern Scotland dedicated to the pursuit of truth in the service of others. The University of Aberdeen became the fifth university in the UK, but our vision remains as strong today as it was then.

Over the centuries, the University has provided excellence in learning, teaching and research, exporting ideas from North East Scotland to the far reaches of the globe. Aberdeen academics and alumni have pioneered many developments in medicine, science, social sciences and humanities, and what is now the University of Aberdeen is associated with five Nobel Laureates.

Today, we are ranked consistently among the top 1% of the world's universities. We offer a broad-based, research-driven centre of excellence attracting academics from the world's most prestigious centres of learning. Our students come from 133 countries, attracted by our heritage, reputation and our enviable record on graduate employment. In terms of graduates, our reach is even bigger with 85,000 graduates in over 170 countries worldwide.

On both King's College and Foresterhill campuses, a multi-million pound development programme is now giving students, staff, and the communities of the city and beyond, unrivalled facilities in which to learn, work and live.

At the same time, a packed and varied programme of lectures, exhibitions, festivals, concerts and informal cafés engage the communities of North East Scotland with exciting research underway at the University on a wide range of topics, and brings leading experts and personalities to the city through a range of events. We also engage with politicians and industry to inform public debate and promote collaborative action to tackle the issues facing society.

Looking to the future, we are determined to enhance our reputation as one of the world's leading universities by moving forward with ever more groundbreaking research; ensuring students have an intellectual and social experience second to none; and capitalising on our dual role as one of the major institutions of the north and as a cornerstone of the economic and cultural life of our region."

It is likely that the crown in the image opposite was incorporated into the architecture to support the Scottish crown's claim to imperial authority within Scotland. It remains the symbolic centre of the ever-growing university campus.

King's College, Old Aberdeen

An Extraordinary Gift

Lewis Grassic Gibbon

Lewis Grassic Gibbon is the pen name of James Leslie Mitchell (1901-1935), the author of Sunset Song, recently voted Scotland's favourite novel.

Dr. William Malcolm's critical analysis of the work of James Leslie Mitchell was published in 1984. He has promoted modern Scottish literature as a teacher, writer, broadcaster and consultant for over three decades -

"James Leslie Mitchell had the humblest of beginnings at the simple crofting house of Hillhead of Seggat in the Aberdeenshire parish of Auchterless where he was born in 1901.

In his teens, he was recognised as a genius at school at Arbuthnott in the Mearns, although there was nothing in his family background to explain where his extraordinary gifts came from.

His fame was hard won, though. After a frustrating year at Mackie Academy in Stonehaven, Mitchell spent short spells unemployed and had a range of jobs – in journalism in Aberdeen and Glasgow, in the forces in the Middle East and in the south of England – before embarking upon a literary career in the south of England in 1929, in Hammersmith and later in Welwyn Garden City.

Amazingly versatile, Mitchell produced seventeen books in his seven year-long writing career, including short story collections, novels, biography and history. His most famous work, however, was written under the pen name of Lewis Grassic Gibbon (an adaptation of his grandmother's name).

Appropriately, his best writing pays tribute to his own roots back home in the North East of Scotland. Sunset Song (1932) rightly wins greatest acclaim as a vibrant tribute to his ain folk, the Scottish peasant crofters who dominated the world in which he had grown up.

The saga continues compellingly through the two succeeding novels in the trilogy A Scots Quair, Cloud Howe (1933) and Grey Granite (1934), respectively following the fortunes of his heroine Chris Guthrie through the Scottish industrial town and the city.

And the short stories collected in Scottish Scene (1934), the miscellany shared with the poet Hugh MacDiarmid, reach the same heights of craftsmanship, especially 'Clay', 'Smeddum', 'Greenden' and 'Forsaken'.

Such an extensive body of work leaves us to ponder sadly what Leslie Mitchell might have gone on to achieve had he not been cut off in his prime, a happy family man not quite thirty four years old, dying of peritonitis after an emergency operation for a stomach ulcer in Queen Victoria Hospital in Welwyn on 7 February 1935.

His ashes now rest in the corner of Arbuthnott Kirkyard, in the heart of the community that shaped his character and provided the raw materials for his greatest writing.

The Grassic Gibbon Centre, set up locally in 1991, symbolises the world-wide fame that Gibbon has won, with stage and media dramatisations of his greatest works having cemented his image as one of Scotland's most iconic writers."

Bloomfield, Childhood Home of Lewis Grassic Gibbon

The Town Is The Venue

Huntly

Huntly is a small market town nestling in the Deveron Valley of western Aberdeenshire.

Cultural heritage is high on Huntly's agenda. Deveron Projects is a significant contributor to this area. Its main aim is to connect artists, communities and places through creative activities.

The framework for Deveron Projects is titled "The Town Is The Venue" where everyone is committed to contribute to the social well-being of Huntly whilst engaging the community in exploring the place through artist-driven projects.

Huntly's small town context, its 18th Century streets and the surrounding Aberdeenshire countryside offers an abundance of artistic opportunities. At the same time, the activities bring people from all walks of life together in public gatherings, symposia, forums, workshops and festivals by being truly inclusive.

Its history is also fascinating. Patrick Scott is a local historian who has written several books on the area including *The History of Strathbogie and The Place-Names of the Parish of Huntly*. Patrick describes Huntly's history -

"Since pre-historical times, the place which we now call Huntly Square has been the focal point of the region that we call Strathbogie. For here are the Stannin Stanes of Strathbogie, part of an ancient stone circle. They are located behind the statue of the Duke of Richmond.

The known history of the town begins with the erection of a castle on the banks of the River Deveron about the year 1180. The family who occupied this castle adopted the name of Strathbogie and remained masters of the strath until 1314 when David of Strathbogie made a monumental mistake!

On the eve of the Battle of Bannockburn, he decided to support Edward of England rather than Robert the Bruce! As a result, David of Strathbogie sought refuge in England and his lands were gifted to Adam Gordon of Huntly in Berwickshire. So began the Gordons long association with Huntly, Aberdeenshire.

The village which grew up in the vicinity of the castle stretched along the old mediaeval road which led from the River Bogie past the castle to the River Deveron. For long it was known as the Raws of Strathbogie or simply Strathbogie. The name Huntly did not become popular until the latter part of the 17th century.

As the Gordon family became more powerful, so did Huntly become more prosperous. In 1488, King James III made the town a free Burgh of Barony. From then on, it became a thriving market town which is still the case today.

The 18th century was a time of great prosperity for the town due to the manufacture of linen and linen goods. About one third of all the linen in Scotland was produced in Huntly and surrounding district.

The mills have long gone but new industries have sprung up. Indeed Dean's shortbread factory has become quite a tourist attraction! And of course each year, tourists walk down the beautiful Linden Avenue (pictured opposite), past the Gordon Schools and Gordon Highlanders' Memorial, to visit the great Castle of Huntly."

The Linden Avenue, Huntly

The Dead Centre Of Aberdeen

Stuart MacBride

With most of his crime novels set in the Granite City, Stuart MacBride is the author of the hugely popular Logan McRae series as well as several other successful novels. *In The Cold Dark Ground* is now his sixth Sunday Times Number 1 bestseller in six years. His novels have sold over two and a half million copies. Stuart has won multiple awards and regularly appears at literary festivals. He describes his favourite part of the city -

"This might sound strange, but I've never set foot inside St. Nicholas Kirk. I lived in Aberdeen most of my life and I've never crossed the threshold. But the graveyard? I've been a regular visitor there since I was a wee boy.

It's always been a favourite shortcut from Union Street to Schoolhill – even though it's quicker to just nip along Back Wynd – walking between those jagged tombstones and looming twisted trees. Maybe whiling away a lunchtime with a Markie's sandwich, on a bench, in the sunshine. Watching the young couples lying on the grass, laughing, and the drunks huddled against the walls, snoring.

There's something wonderfully restful about having that calm, green space in the middle of Union Street. A break from the hustle and press of shoppers. The diesel rumble of bendy-buses muffled by the dirty granite pillars of its façade.

I have no idea when I first walked the crooked path that hooks around the side of the kirk, but I can't have been more than three or four: a wee boy, my dad holding my hand so I wouldn't run off to play with the headstones.

And then he stopped, and pointed at the granite slab beneath our feet. The writing carved into its surface was faded, scuffed almost smooth by generations of Aberdonian shoes, just like all the other granite slabs that form a large proportion of the path. And then my father said, "Did you know you're standing on dead people?"

That freaked the living hell out me at the time. I still mutter, "Excuse me…" whenever I walk along that path, apologising to the deceased as my shoes scuff away a little more of their legacy.

Of course, we don't call it St. Nicholas Kirk, do we? Not unless we're being posh or polite. No, to most Aberdonians it's The Dead Centre, sitting where it does and containing what it does. Now to me, that's the perfect title for a crime novel, but for some strange reason I haven't managed to write it yet.

I did manage to get the graveyard into one of my books, though – I set a fundraising charity concert for a kidnapped mother and daughter there – but one of these days I'm definitely going to have a dead body discovered in one of the kirk's pews. I suppose then I'll have to break the habit of a lifetime and actually go inside."

St. Nicholas Kirkyard, Aberdeen

An Ecological Success Story

The River Don

Rising in the Cairngorms National Park and flowing 135km in an easterly direction towards the sea in Aberdeen, the Don is Scotland's sixth largest river. It is famous for its salmon and particularly its brown trout fishing.

Donside is stunning in autumn and takes on different photogenic characteristics throughout the seasons. Most people will see the River Don as pleasant, peaceful and rural but this hasn't always been the case for the whole river, particularly in the lower section as it nears its estuary in the north of the city. The history of the Don has been beset with pollution problems for which solutions have been sought over the years.

Robert Dey, Chair of the River Don Trust, expands on some of the historical challenges that have been overcome to create the attractive and ecologically sustainable habitat that the river has become today -

"From the 18th century, the river became heavily industrialised in its lower four miles with three paper mills, cotton and cloth mills and a pork processing factory which cumulatively led to the lower river becoming grossly polluted. Another paper mill upriver at Inverurie also added to the problem. The upper Don was famed for the quality of its brown trout fishing but the lower river was devoid of life.

In the 20th century, the concoction of sewage deposited in the tidal stretches of the river made living in the vicinity of the Don estuary very unpleasant when the tide went out as the mud flats gave off a strong smell, especially bad in summer months.

In the 1960s, there were complaints by the residents and in the early 1970s, a public meeting arranged by Aberdeen & District Angling Association was held in the Aberdeen Music Hall to protest about the conditions in the lower river. The North East River Purification Board and the mill owners were invited to attend and were urged to take steps to clean up the river. New waste treatment facilities costing several millions of pounds were, over time, introduced. It eventually became the case that the waste water leaving the mills was actually cleaner than when it came out of the river.

Gradually, the condition of the river improved and, over the years, most of the mills causing the pollution have closed down one by one. The black contaminated mud flats in the estuary have gone and the tidal area is now free of the unpleasant odours of the past. The lower river is nowadays a clean, healthy environment with a diverse range of insects, fish and other wildlife."

The image opposite is of early morning light on a stretch of the River Don between Monymusk and Keig. Autumn on Donside is a riot of colour and a dream for photographers as the river follows its serpentine route towards the sea, often with the Mither Tap of Bennachie providing an unexpected backdrop.

The River Don at Keig, near Alford

Founder Of Modern Japan

Thomas Blake Glover

One of the most important figures in the history of modern Japan was born in the North East of Scotland. Thomas Blake Glover's contribution to the creation of industrial prosperity in Japan is recognised throughout the length and breadth of the Land of the Rising Sun. He is, however, less well-known in his native land.

Hamish Vernal, past Provost of Aberdeenshire, has a particular interest in exploring some of the area's "forgotten heroes" who are less well-known in the land of their birth than in the countries where they have had significant influence and are much revered, one of whom is Glover -

"Thomas Blake Glover was born in the coastal town of Fraserburgh. His father, a Londoner, was Chief Coastguard Officer in the town, his mother was a Banffshire lass from Fordyce. His home was only 100 metres from the busy fishing and trading harbour and close to the sand dunes and rocky foreshore. These early years spent in an environment full of maritime and trading influences helped mould his later dramatic career.

In 1851, the family moved to the Bridge of Don in Aberdeen where Thomas completed his education. He could rightly be described as a "lad o' pairts". Using his education together with his adventurous and entrepreneurial spirit, he set out across the world to find "fame and fortune".

He entered employment with the trading company of Jardine Matheson and volunteered, in 1859, to go to Japan as a trader and an agent, this at a time when feudal Japan was resisting Western attempts to open the country to trade.

His political adeptness paid off. Siding with the new anti-feudal regime, he became involved in several risky ventures and adventures. He was known as Guraba in Japan and took a Japanese wife.

After the new regime was established, Thomas was set to become immersed in the industry of Japan. He introduced the first railway, he purchased the first ships for the Japanese Navy, which were built in Hall's shipyard in Aberdeen. He founded businesses which became Mitsubishi and the Kirin Brewery companies in Nagasaki. He also developed Japan's first coal mine and the country's first dry dock.

Thomas Blake Glover is much revered in Japan as the founder of the industrialised period in Japan's history. He was given the Honour of the Rising Sun and because of this and his adventures in the military coup became known as the "Scottish Samurai".

He is commemorated greatly in Japan and the Glover Garden in Nagasaki is visited annually by two million visitors. The family home in Fraserburgh no longer exists, having been bombed during World War 2; however, there is a large section dedicated to Thomas Blake Glover in the Fraserburgh Heritage Museum and a dedicated museum in Fraserburgh's oldest house, Warld's End.

It is fitting that there are now plans to convert the Glover House in Aberdeen into an Innovation Hub. Thomas would have approved!!!"

Glover House, Bridge of Don

Stonehaven Open Air Pool

An Art Deco Jewel

In the early seventies, all of my leisure time was spent at the Stonehaven Open Air Pool. It was the only place to be for a teenager in the summer months.

In later life, as a photographer, I grew to appreciate the Pool as a wonderful example of art deco architecture. The bold bright colours and geometric shapes are a testimony to the imagination of the architects.

The Friends of Stonehaven Open Air Swimming Pool have a major role to play in ensuring that it enjoys continuing success -

"Stonehaven Swimming Pool was built and opened before the Second World War. Today it is one of only two which survive from that era and the North of Scotland's only open air pool. It is the UK's only Olympic-size, heated, seawater, open air, art deco swimming pool!

When it opened in 1934, the Pool was funded by the Stonehaven public. It was emptied every few days and filled again with unheated water from the nearby North Sea. By the following season, it had a basic heating, filtration and disinfection system and its popularity grew steadily. However, the availability of cheap package holidays to the Mediterranean led to its decline and by the 1990s, it was threatened with closure as part of a council cost-saving exercise.

The Friends of Stonehaven Open Air Swimming Pool was founded at that time as a community pressure group which succeeded in saving the Pool for future generations. Using the voluntary professional and trade skills – and labour – of its members, it transformed the Pool from a drain on council funds to a jewel in the crown of Aberdeenshire.

Now "The Friends", a registered Charity, works in close partnership with Aberdeenshire Council which owns, staffs and operates the facility. The Friends' role is to maintain, enhance and promote the pool as an attraction for visitors from near and far and, of course, for residents of Stonehaven and the surrounding area. The Friends still rely on the skills and labour of their volunteer workforce to keep the Pool looking its best.

Today, the Pool's safe, treated seawater is heated to a balmy 29°C/85°F – warmer than most of the Mediterranean for much of the summer! Open from late May until early September each year, it provides splashy, healthy fun for all ages and, at a little more than 50m long, it can provide a real workout for serious swimmers including Olympic swimmer and Commonwealth gold medal winner David Carry who has used the pool for training purposes.

The chute is breathtakingly fast, there are fun sessions for kids at specific times and quiet swims at others. It is an ideal picnic spot although the on-site café also sells tasty hot and cold snacks and drinks. In high season, you can 'swim beneath the stars' at weekly midnight swims and the sun terraces, with loungers and patio furniture, can be sheltered sunbathing heaven!"

Stonehaven Open Air Pool

A Royal Paradise

Balmoral Castle

Balmoral Castle has been the Scottish home of the Royal Family since it was purchased for Queen Victoria by Prince Albert in 1852.

In the autumn of 1842, two and a half years after her marriage to Prince Albert, Queen Victoria paid her first visit to Scotland. They were so struck with the Highlands that they resolved to return. A further visit to Perthshire and then Ardverikie encouraged them to seize the opportunity to purchase Balmoral.

After searching enquiries, they bought Balmoral Estate on the 17th of February 1848 and on the 8th of September 1848, they arrived to take possession of a property they had never seen. They were not disappointed and when they returned south, they opened negotiations for the purchase of the land on which Balmoral stood.

These protracted negotiations were completed on the 22nd of June 1852 when Balmoral was purchased by Prince Albert. Once the land was purchased, they decided to rebuild as the building was no longer adequate for their needs. The architect selected was William Smith, City Architect of Aberdeen. Soon after the family arrived at the castle, Mr Smith was summoned.

Prince Albert decided to build a new castle as the current one was considered not large enough for the Royal Family. A new site was chosen, 100 yards to the north west of the building, so that they could continue to occupy the old house while the new castle was under construction.The foundation stone for Balmoral Castle was laid by Queen Victoria on the 28th of September 1853 and can be found at the foot of the wall adjacent to the west face of the entrance porch.

Before the foundation stone was placed in position, Queen Victoria signed a parchment recording the date. This parchment, together with an example of each of the current coins of the realm, was then placed in a bottle and inserted into a cavity below the site prepared for the stone. The castle was completed in 1856 and the old building was then demolished.

When Queen Victoria died in 1901, Balmoral Estates passed, under the terms of her will, to King Edward VII and from him to each of his successors. Although it remains largely the same as it was in Queen Victoria's reign, successive royal owners have followed the initiative of Prince Albert in making improvements to the estate. The Queen, The Duke of Edinburgh and The Prince of Wales take a close personal interest in running and improving the Estates.

In her journals, Queen Victoria described Balmoral as *"my dear paradise in the Highlands"*.

Balmoral Castle in Springtime

Artisans and Academics

Old Aberdeen

Old Aberdeen is hidden away in the north of the city but it has an important history and an identity of its own. Primarily, these days, it is the home of Aberdeen University but there is a lot more to be discovered in its cobbled streets and fascinating vennels.

Old Aberdeen can be loosely divided into three areas. The oldest part is known as the Chanonry situated around St Machar's Cathedral which was founded in the 12th Century. This area grew in parallel with the development of the Cathedral.

In 1489, Old Aberdeen was granted a charter by King James IV and became a Burgh of Barony. From this period, the merchant area around the Town House evolved. The academic sector developed after the foundation of King's College in 1495.

David Parkinson is Ex Deacon Convener of The Seven Incorporated Trades of Aberdeen. Here he explains the relevance of the area to the ancient trades of Old Aberdeen -

"Take as a starting point the Old Town House in Old Aberdeen, once the administrative centre where court was held. In the past, it has also served as a church mission, masonic lodge, jail and a library.

Facing the market square, proceed down the High Street towards Kings College Chapel and on the left you will find Wrights' and Coopers' Place which is pictured opposite. It is named after one of the incorporated trades of Old Aberdeen and is made up of simple single-storey cottages, providing a stark contrast to the grand Georgian town houses nearby.

Wrights, who were workers in wood, and Coopers, who were barrel makers, may have lived and worked in this area. Their trade organisation, along with others in the Old Aberdeen Incorporated Trades, owned and feued property throughout the area.

The Wrights were made up of craftsmen; these included wheelwrights, millwrights, cartwrights, shipwrights and housewrights, woodturners, carvers and cabinetmakers.

The Coopers represented the barrel makers who not only made various sizes of barrels for the breweries and distillers, but mainly provided barrels for the fishing industry and the storage and packaging of herring.

The area was restored in 1965 for the University, financed by the MacRobert Trust. In the same year, Robert Hurd and Partners, the architects who restored Grant's Place, created the MacRobert Memorial Garden at the end of Wrights' and Coopers' Place.

As part of the memorial garden, a granite wall was built containing the names of Lady MacRobert's three sons who fell in service during the Second World War, along with a mosaic that presents the family coat of arms "Not For Themselves But For Their Native Land".

Old Aberdeen was originally a completely separate place from New Aberdeen whose development started at Castle Hill and around the harbour area. Eventually Old Aberdeen was absorbed into the city of Aberdeen."

Wrights' and Coopers' Place, Old Aberdeen

When The Heron Leaves The Tree

Gight Castle

Gight Castle is an ivy-covered characterful ruin four miles east of Fyvie. Lord Aberdeen, whose family owns the castle, tells its colourful story -

"It is not possible to be precise about the exact date that Gight Castle was constructed but it is likely to be in the mid to late 15th Century.

The branch of Aberdeenshire Gordons who first occupied the castle in the 1490s descended from the 2nd Earl of Huntly and his wife Princess Annabella, a daughter of King James 1st of Scotland. Through thirteen successive generations, their behaviour left a lot to be desired and they were particularly violent both towards neighbours and those further afield.

A notorious incident occurred during the tenure of the 7th Laird in the 1640s during the period of the Covenanters. In the knowledge that his castle would be sieged and sacked, he gathered all his silver and fine linen and threw them into the pool of the River Ythan at the bottom of the brae known as the Hagberry Pot. When the danger had passed, the Laird sent a diver down to retrieve his treasure. He returned ashen-faced to say he had witnessed the Devil having a tea party and would not descend again. After gentle persuasion – known to most as torture – he went down again and, with a great swirling of the water, surfaced with a fork through his heart. No one knows what became of the treasure.

The last laird of this line was Catherine Gordon who succeeded in 1779. She married the extravagant wastrel "Mad" Jack Byron who quickly ran through her considerable fortune. She was forced to sell her estate to the 3rd Earl of Aberdeen from neighbouring Haddo. Her son, George, the great poet and later Lord Byron, never lived at Gight and was born in London but never forgave his neighbours for depriving him of his inheritance.

Thomas the Rhymer had predicted that "when the heron leaves the tree, the Laird of Gight will landless be". For years, herons had nested at Gight but flew to Haddo thereby proving the prophesy right. The castle was then occupied by the 3rd Earl's son, Lord Haddo, and his young family. Sadly, he was to die in a riding accident in 1791 and his widow then left for London with her six children and the castle has remained unoccupied ever since."

International percussionist Dame Evelyn Glennie, who was brought up on a farm near neighbouring Methlick, fondly remembers her childhood visits to the castle - *"My favourite part of Aberdeenshire is Gight Castle which is very close to the family farm and where I used to cycle and walk to and roll eggs when little. It's a ruin but used to be such an exciting place to go to as a youngster."*

Gight Castle, Methlick

Elemental Wilderness

Lochnagar

Lochnagar is situated near Balmoral Castle on Royal Deeside. It has featured on film in Mrs. Brown, in the children's story of the Old Man of Lochnagar, written by the Prince of Wales, and in a famous poem by Lord Byron. It is a popular mountain for walkers and climbers but, in hostile weather conditions, many have become stranded and have required the skills of the Mountain Rescue service.

Malcolm Duckworth has spent many years active in mountain rescue. He is a mountaineer, an instructor, an International Mountain Leader and a photographer who has climbed in many parts of the world including arctic Alaska.

Malcolm describes the experience of being on Lochnagar at night to rescue a climber and of being at one with the mountain -

"We crossed the col to the west of Meikle Pap and descended into the corrie of Lochnagar. The moon shadow had plunged the corrie into impenetrable blackness. Traversing the snow aprons below the cliffs, we headed for our climb, head torches bobbing in the dark. We cut steps into Raeburn's Gully, his ghost laughing at our bold impertinence. 600ft, defying gravity, on snow and ice in this chasm that split the cliffs and the moon found us again as we emerged onto the plateau. The lunar light turned the landscape into sheets of frozen satin.

I knew that sub-zero February night that this mountain, with its extremes of moods, would draw me back for the rest of my mountaineering career.

Years later, we traced the same route in the dying light of a winter's day to rescue an injured climber, the snow whirling madly as we lowered him from iced cliffs to the base of the corrie. An ancient RAF Rescue Whirlwind, its searchlight bouncing crazily in the wind, located us and winched the casualty up. Seconds later, the clattering rotors were swallowed by the weather and we were in darkness with a million spinning snowflakes.

Lochnagar features in the photography, art, poetry and writings of many people. It is a mountain for all. Its high plateau attracts walkers while the rock architecture of its cliffs entices the summer rock and winter ice climbers.

Summer has removed the winter's shell revealing the rock architecture and has released its soundtrack. Above us, a 650ft rock equation of grooves, chimneys, and knife edges; the algebra of Eagle Ridge. Karabiners and ropes aid the solution connecting us physically to the climb.

But there exists a deeper bond that resonates with the rhythm of the mountain and connects to our DNA. We scramble the final slab, pack our gear and mingle with the crowds and the less esoteric world of the plateau.

I have stood on that high icy plateau in that elemental wilderness and watched the sky dipping to indigo, the horizon tinged terracotta, the stars lighting one by one, and sensed how small we are in the infinity."

Towards Lochnagar from Ballater

Scotland's Favourite Novel

Sunset Song

Published in 1932, Sunset Song is the story of Chris Guthrie, a young girl growing up in a close-knit farming community in the Mearns, an area of the ancient county of Kincardineshire in the south of Aberdeenshire. Written by Lewis Grassic Gibbon, it is set in the lead-up to and the outbreak of the First World War. It explores Chris's coming of age and the turmoil of change that is happening around her in every aspect of her young life.

It deals with broad themes such as change, morality, man's relationship with the land, the role of women, in particular Chris's increasing independence as she moves into womanhood, the character of a close-knit community, the loss of the old farming ways and the brutalising and dehumanising consequences of war.

It stands out as a masterpiece in Scottish Literature and has been voted as Scotland's favourite book. It is also the favourite novel of Scotland's First Minister, Nicola Sturgeon, who championed the book at the time of the vote -

"I first read Sunset Song when I was in my teens, maybe thirteen or fourteen, and it resonated with me firstly because it was a wonderful story, beautifully written, but it also said something about the country that I grew up in. I think its themes are timeless to this day."

Sunset Song contains my own favourite piece from Scottish Literature. Coming at the end of the novel, Grassic Gibbon defines, through his choice and use of language, the character of North East Scotland in his description of the memorial service to the four young men from Kinraddie who had lost their lives in the Great War, including Ewan Tavendale, Chris's husband.

The parishioners are gathered on the hillside listening to the words of the Reverend Colquhoun -

"For I Will Give You The Morning Star. In the sunset of an age and an epoch we may write that for epitaph of the men who were of it. They went quiet and brave from the lands they loved, though seldom of that love might they speak, it was not in them to tell in words of the earth that moved and lived and abided, their life and enduring love. And who knows at the last what memories of it were with them, the springs and the winters of this land and all the sounds and scents of it that had once been theirs, deep, and a passion of their blood and spirit, those four who died in France?"

As I reach the conclusion of this new perspective on the North East of Scotland, it is the vivid colour and texture of an Aberdeenshire sky that I would like to have as my penultimate image - a sunset above the fields of Arbuthnott, the fictional Kinraddie in Sunset Song.

Every time I see a sunset like this in the Mearns, I think of Chris Guthrie.

A Mearns Sunset

Aberdeenshire's Cape Cod

Journey's End

My final image represents the end of a journey for me with this book. It has been a journey of celebration of some of the most stunning landscapes and seascapes that I have ever photographed, often in an exceptional quality of light. I have rediscovered a vibrant and dynamic city with elegant classical and imaginative contemporary architecture. I have been reminded of a unique cultural identity and some amazing personal achievements. I have discovered a depth of talent in all its forms.

In the course of **Aberdeen**shire - A New Perspective, I have immersed myself visually in my local area and have come to realise how special a place it is. If I had to choose one moment of photographic epiphany from the whole project, it was one evening standing by myself on the beach at Rattray Head, in complete silence, looking south at low tide in the last hour of an April day.

As I began to absorb the scene in front of me, a thought entered my head that the year before, I visited Cape Cod in Massachusetts, a beautiful part of the United States, rightly famed for its beaches and a place of pilgrimage for photographers from all over the world, myself included.

But what I witnessed that evening in glorious golden light, a few miles south of Fraserburgh, was the equal of anything that I saw on Cape Cod. The quality of light was out of this world. Cape Cod is 3,000 miles from Aberdeen, Rattray Head is 40 miles away.

For people living or working in the North East, it is all there on our doorsteps. For visitors to the area, it is definitely worth taking a few more days than you had originally intended to explore the city of Aberdeen and Aberdeenshire.

I was recently asked by an organisation to try to distil what it was that made the North East of Scotland special and different from other places. I concluded that the difference is in the difference. There is no single feature to set it apart. Its uniqueness is in its diversity.

But the essential component for me is its people - indigenous people who have lived in the North East all their lives, people who have come to work and have settled or visitors who resolve to return year after year. I have met many people from all three categories in the course of this project.

If people are the essence of the area, I am reminded of the motto of the City of Aberdeen which is equally true of Aberdeenshire -

"Happy to meet, sorry to part, happy to meet again."

Rattray Head, Buchan Coast

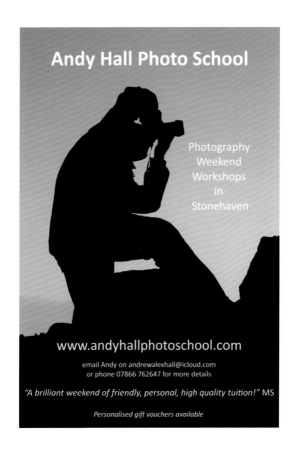

Prints from the **Aberdeen**shire - A New Perspective collection are available to purchase.
Please contact Andy on andrewalexhall@icloud.com

Images from elsewhere in Scotland, New York City, Santorini and Iceland can be seen on
Andy's website

www.andyhallphotography.com